ELEVATING
wisdom
on the *walk*

compiled by **lori l. dixon** Ed.S.

featuring

NIKI BANNING • CRYSTAL DUNCAN-HOGUE
FRANCISCA ETUOKWU-BENYEOGOR
MANTEQUILLA GREEN • TINA JACOBSON
NATALIE MERRILL

Book design by Callie Revell, callierevell.com

Published by LLD Legacy Publishing, LLC

Printed in the United States of America

dedication

In this book, I was not planning on writing a chapter. Instead, I wanted the women I am blessed to be surrounded by to be honored with their own writing. But, God shifted many of the authors, which opened the door for me to write about "legacy" and why it has become a spotlighted piece of my life.

I do believe it is for many of you reading these words today. I pray you will be intrigued, supported, inspired, and called as you digest the very words these women have placed on the page, as well as the ones I am sharing just for you.

To my adopted mom, Loretta Lane-Christiansen—When my mom passed in 2013, she was the last remaining person in our family's immediate history. What does that mean? She carried and knew the stories of my adoptive childhood, her childhood, my dad's and her life, my sister's memories and legacies that were not carried forward anywhere else but with ME!

At mom's memorial lunch at our church in Florida, I hugged, reminisced, and heard the stories of her life with her friends and what they remembered of my life growing up in Clearwater. Mom treasured friends and family. She treasured life and love in a BIG way, and I was blessed to watch her do the very actions of celebrating life and laughter.

As we all sat around the table at a favorite restaurant sharing, crying, laughing, and loving, I shared how Mom's legacy was around BOOKS and stories. Her friends and I decided to purchase and donate books to libraries and schools with my mom's name within them.

Mom raised me to love books, and we shared many of them together. We both had extensive libraries of books for all ages, including children's books that we both would purchase for each other at different holidays and inscribe a beautiful memory and rationale as to why we knew the other person would LOVE the storyline. Most of those books are still a part of my own library and I still purchase books for friends and extended friends and family.

This love of books translated into writing stories together, Mom and I, and now publishing them for others to read and be inspired. Mom would be so proud. It is with this book, *Elevating the Wisdom on the Walk*, I dedicate to my mom's love of the Lord and her passion for books.

Aunt Lois O'Neal—P.S... as I write this dedication to legacy and to writing, my precious Aunt Lois, who was like a second mother to me, is transitioning to Heaven. I know in my spirit she will be met at the gates of Heaven and the streets of gold with all the family that has gone on before us, including my Mom, Dad, sister, and biological sister, Jody, and her husbands, parents, and siblings, too. I know in my heart, they are sharing stories together of exactly where they left off, chatting and laughing. The updates of the lives of those who remaining here will long be discussed for many days to come.

It is for each of them that I dedicate the stories within this book, and especially my own chapter of LEGACY, which is meant to honor each of them.

May YOU be blessed through the writing of each chapter you will read. You are having a glimpse of a beautiful life of a Christian, faith-filled woman, the legacies that went on before them, and their memories to be honored by many.

appreciation

I want to honor the legacies of:

My sister, Jody Glass, and her direction in the expansion of my faith and understanding of the Lord.

My aunt, Lois O'Neal, who poured into my life from an early age and showed me the path of being dedicated to the Lord in all you do.

My mom, Loretta Lane, who supported my passion for writing and reading as well as studying the Bible and deepening faith.

I want to honor the legacies in the making of the following and the individual entrusted to carry them:

Niki Banning—bestie, sister in the faith, lead editor, and story coach (guardian), right hand to all things in our work and outreach, talented and blessed with gifts she readily shares with our authors, collaborators, and team.

Callie Revell—sister in the faith, publishing and social media assistant, walks in faith and grace.

Shelby Gonzalez — sister in the faith, Team WoW leader, creation and ideation in our work and life, blessing in the inner circle and supports us through actions and prayers.

Tanya Rivera, one of my precious nieces—pastor and apostle to the Lord's work, carries the legacy of faith and outreach, ministers to us and draws us closer to the Lord.

contents

introduction

Lori L. Dixon, Ed.S.

Welcome to Wisdom on the Walk, where women's faith-inspired journeys of life are shared to ignite your own through revealing, embracing, and now elevating the truth of God, His Kingdom, and rippling circles of influence and impact to others.

Our mission and vision scriptures have created a strong platform for women of faith and their stories.

> And the Lord answered me and said, Write the vision and engrave it so plainly upon tablets that everyone who passes may (be able to) read (it easily and quickly) as he/she hastens by.
>
> Habakkuk 2:2 (AMP)

And…

> The Lord gives the word (of power); the women who bear and publish (the news) are great hosts.
>
> Psalms 68:11 (AMP)

God has given us the assignment. We accept it and are carrying it out diligently in His Name.

I welcome you to the WoW… Wisdom on the Walk!

Let me introduce myself to you.

Bringing four decades of wisdom and experience into the work God has led me to is a whole new adventure. I am a prophetic visionary, or some would say a "seer" for the Lord. I am also a Kingdom entrepreneur bringing forth the "ah-ha" for and with others for their life assignments and callings.

Previously I have been a multiple international award-winning host and producer on streaming and linear TV with Zondra TV Network. While working on Bravo's *Real Housewives of Dallas* with some of my fabulous celebrity clients, I learned about the further "realities" of how chapters of our lives may be rewritten at any time.

As a Christian faith leader, I am a best-selling author, transformational speaker, media personality, and a Christian story navigator, best-selling publisher, and marketing supporter. Founding Walk with Lori to bring forth healing and faith experiences and opportunities, and LLD Legacy Publishing and LLD Legacy Ministries to be vehicles for mission and ministry for Kingdom women and their stories are all companies I lead daily.

Every day I look at the wall behind my desk, I see the letters… WoW, and I remember its meaning and importance in my life and the lives of others!

Every day I look at life in the faces of those around me, interact with powerful women of the faith, and create shared discussions of faith, I say... WoW, and I remember its meaning and importance in my life and the lives of others!

Every day I look at the beauty surrounding us of the breathtaking sunsets, flowing waters, budding trees, sensational sand, majestic majesty of the mountains, I believe in the WoW, and I remember its meaning and importance in my life and the lives of others!

Every day I look at the words on a page that someone has written that was inspired by the Lord and guided by His Holy Spirit, I hear the WoW, and I remember its meaning and importance in my life and the lives of others!

Every day I look at what the Lord has created, and I appreciate the WoW and I remember its meaning and importance in my life and the lives of others!

Where does the WoW appear in your life?

Where does God show you the WoW and how do you accept it?

What IS the WoW for you?

THIS is the third book in the series of the WoW journey. We have included the stories of 34 women and rippled out to launches that attracted over 450 people and both books have been best-sellers. God is truly doing something amidst all this action in His name!

The progression of the books has gone from "Revealing" the Wisdom on the Walk with the Lord to "Embracing" the WoW, to the newest being "Elevating" the WoW. This edition shares the deeper stories of seven women and a new feature we are very excited about, "scripture mapping" and a companion journal entitled, "Deepening Your WoW" to enhance the opportunities for bible study and book studies.

Can't you see the experience of reading a chapter, mapping the scriptures included to "elevate" your wisdom with the Lord on your own walk? That is a WoW!

Every chapter will feature an author's story, quotes for highlighting, a prayer, reflection questions, and now a scripture map of a focus verse that inspired the author. Then, pages for you to reflect and map the same scripture or an additional one found within the story.

Every day the Lord expands the meaning of the WoW, and we are blessed.

Every day the Lord asks us to deepen our WoW with Him.

Every day we include new women seeking for community in our Wisdom on the Walk Author group.

I ask you, "will you?" How will you elevate the EVERY DAY?

Be blessed, Be Bold, Be YOU, dear ones...

walking in legacy

Lori L. Dixon, Ed.S.

Today you have [openly] declared the LORD to be your God, and that you will walk [that is, live each and every day] in His ways and keep His statutes, His commandments, and His judgments (precepts), and listen to His voice. Today the LORD has declared that you are His people, His treasured possession, just as He promised you, and that you are to keep all His commandments; and that He will set you high above all the nations which He has made, for praise, fame, and honor: and that you shall be a holy people [set apart and consecrated] to the LORD your God, just as He has spoken.

Deuteronomy 26:17-19 (AMP)

What does legacy mean to you? Perhaps birthright comes to mind. Do you think about what has been passed down to you, like the way I think about my grandmother's delicate and decorative china from Denmark? Maybe to you, it's the recent trend of those seeking identity through places such as 23 and Me or Ancestry.com. Or do you look at it as bloodline and as the Biblical "sins of the fathers" reference? Take a moment and reflect below on what legacy means to you. It may be some or even "all of the above."

For me, legacy has always meant family. And that thought was strengthened as I began having family members passing away—especially my father when I was 25. Carrying on the family name held for me a way to preserve what being adopted and having the family name of "Lane" with all of its cultural heritage meant. I even use the L. for Lane, my maiden name, as my middle name to carry what their acceptance, love, support, and caring meant to me.

When my adoptive mom passed away in 2013, my newest business was being formed. I named the business LLD Legacy to honor her wisdom, laughter, love, and to carry her life lessons forward with me. As I started writing again and speaking, I created LLD Legacy Publishing in my parents' honor.

Little did I know what the Lord had planned for this work. He began revealing His plans in 2023 when I found the next step in the journey to writing and publishing through legacy again. When my biological family, which included my precious sister, Jody Glass, walked into my life, my identity was complete—but not in the way you may think.

Through this new relationship and connection, I learned my stories around family, siblings, history, my adoption, and more. Yet, the Lord had a different, underlying surprise that would surface when I was ready. As I grew in my closeness with my family, I drew closer to understanding at a deeper level my relationship with God and especially Christ. I looked at who I was with so much more clarity, and the beauty I saw in my own "story" surfaced. It also helped that my sister was a pastor and apostle, and my own prophetic gifts were now realized and understood. Jody took me under her wing and pulled me in close to her and the Lord. What a safe space to be! This legacy mattered and would matter forever.

> For Yahweh is always good and ready to receive you. He's so loving that it will amaze you—so kind that it will astound you! Everyone knows our God can be trusted, for He keeps his promises to every generation.
>
> Psalm 100:5 (TPT)

We have the utmost pleasure and privilege to have God as our Father, no matter where we came from.

He is our Creator of all and so much more. His identities are vast so He can nurture and provide exactly what is needed in His perfect time and even place in our lives.

I love how, in Numbers 3 and 4, Moses receives how to acknowledge, identify, and "number" God's people and what tasks they will be assigned. Why would the Lord ask Moses to record every tribe and household, having them listed and numbered along with every son and every offspring? Why would He designate certain roles and responsibilities to different families and households?

Lineage was important to create clarity and order, not chaos and confusion. As the lands were populated there were to be rules and laws. Not to "rule over" and dictate, but for paths outlayed to be followed and honored. It is how lands were assigned and communities were built. All in the blueprint of the great Creator, God. Later in the prophets' writings, we see how the lineage of Jesus would be tied to the young David and his family, who would later become a great king for the shifts of God's precious people.

It is such a blessing to be adopted, chosen, and cherished in the Lord's family. What a legacy in itself! No matter what type of family we were born and raised in, God accepts us and loves us dearly. He is our ABBA Father, and His identity is just being realized in this life. When we accept Christ as our Savior and God as our Father, we become a living testimony and legacy IN HIM.

> "No matter what type of family we were born and raised in, God accepts us and loves us dearly."
>
> *lori l. dixon*

Belonging was my first lesson as an adopted child. Belonging in a family I wasn't born into and taking a new name that may have been, but probably was not the one I was given at birth. Yet, the Lord was with me at a very young age as I sensed His presence and words to me and to be shared with others. He gave me visions and prompted me to bring messages of love, compassion, and His truth for all of us.

Research tells us that adopted children may experience a loss of belonging, a sense of abandonment, and even sometimes a reluctance to connect with their adoptive families and others. God needed me to continue learning through my life about identity and what being in a family and participating as a sister, daughter, niece, and child of a legacy meant.

I remember what funny a thing being *in* a legacy can be—and you may relate. Yes, I was a child born in the 1960s when telephones and cords were still connected to a wall in most homes. As a young child of four years, my mother taught me the first lesson of telephone etiquette. My dad was in the higher ranks of the military and oftentimes took very important and confidential calls from other military leaders and political officials. My responsibility was to answer the telephone within the first two rings—often a feat of running through the house to catch the receiver, and trying not to appear out of breath. Then, to answer with the phrase of "Lane residence, Lori speaking." That was a lot for a four year old! Once executing that greeting, I was to either take a message, handwritten on special paper notes by the phone, or find my father and bring him quickly to the phone and share who was on the other line. Wow! Yes, they placed great trust in my abilities at a young age.

This continued even into adulthood as I would answer my parents' and eventually just my mother's phone. That was how I realized the beginning of my legacy and belonging within the family.

Belonging is an essential component of legacy. As humans, we are created by the Divine to seek connection and community, always finding our way back to Him. Yet, I encounter the need for belonging, boundaries, loss, and grief healing tools and strategies with my therapeutic coaching clients on a regular basis. I find our desire to remain in closely linked relationships is frequently sabotaged by our own inner lack of what we have had with God. It creates in us a constant seeking.

I, myself, am all too familiar with the loss of loving relationships and starting to learn at an early age of five how this disconnection and grief affects how we relate with others. As I grappled with what loss means in our legacy of life, God revealed to me a new understanding

"In the silence, I could hear their voices and feel their divine presence sitting with me. I knew my tears were being collected and valued by my Father."

lori l dixon

again in my own grief and loss of eight important relationships during 2024. I learned to not ask "why," but to ease into the pain, feel all that I could feel, and continue to stay open to experiencing life. The Lord nurtured me and the Holy Spirit comforted me through this difficult time. In the silence, I could hear their voices and feel their divine presence sitting with me. I knew my tears were being collected and valued by my Father.

One scripture I held onto at an early age as a Christian was in Psalm 30:5 (NIV): "Tears may flow through the night, but JOY comes in the morning." When I was in fifth grade, our confirmation class received Bibles in the front of the church. It was then I found through the Psalms, the comforts and compassions of the Lord for David and the legacy David carried in the Lord. As a youth in Christ, it nurtured me.

Facing death and loss was difficult, and those words entered my spirit to cling to forever. We do have those nights and sometimes days, but the Lord promises He is there with us through it and He hears our cries. Our tears matter to him. Our *joy* in Him is one of His greatest desires for us.

Sometimes we hear people talk about the baggage we carry in life—the hurts, the fears, the traumas, and the loss. We, as Christians, know God is the God of the "light load," which means He wants us to give our baggage and burdens to Him and walk forward in His truth and light. True joy isn't experienced in the milestone mentality where we say, "if I can only…," it is found in the daily walk with the Lord. Each step He brings us to and through teaches us to trust and walk in faith with Him.

My "baggage" over the years could have been extremely heavy, and at times it was. When I would try to drag my unpacked and emotionally filled moments and memories, it only brought deep pain, grief, and questions to help my ill-equipped actions to support those family members and friends involved. Who was I to assist them when I didn't feel I had the tools myself?

After the sudden passing of my father, my mom leaned into me, and my role and responsibility shifted. I was in my mid-twenties and newly married. Mom was navigating her way without her life partner and the love of her life. She found joy and solace in her faith and modeled for all of us how to walk through grief as a Christian woman. Yes, one of those lessons was to be there and honor my mom over the years as she leaned hard on me and gave me the responsibility of being there for her. From my early twenties until my late 30s, I carried my baggage—and sometimes hers, too.

During a major transition of life in my 30s, I found myself divorced and working on the demands of an advanced degree, my PhD. Working, being there for mom, and even dating was a full-time life.

My sister, Susie, lived with her family in Illinois, and mom and I were Florida residents. One profound day as I drove home after some intense course sessions, my brother-in-law called my cell phone (yes, we had them by then). His news was not what any of us could imagine. Susie had passed away suddenly. We were all stunned and quite numb. I drove quickly to see my mom to unfortunately deliver the devastating news to her. Her daughter was now in Heaven with Dad.

Susie's legacy was in her grandchildren, and that would remain. The stories still were ingrained in us and, as you know, sharing them, laughing about them, and treasuring the memories is what is constant. As Christians, we knew it was about giving our grief to the Lord and letting Him carry it for us. But for me, even in doing so, it left a profound ache in my heart and soul. Nothing would be as it was—and that was a truth we had to carry.

You can imagine how my mom changed. Her connection and need for me to be there with her, or at least know each day where I was, became extremely important. There was a fear growing within her that she would be completely alone without me. Mom clung to her faith, staying in a state of joy, and thankful for friends around her.

It wasn't until I met my husband that I began to dig in deep and question my own baggage, coming into the marriage and defining my actions and purpose in life. Was I a victim—hurt and bruised by grief? Or was I a victor in Christ, who took away my sin and the pain I carried for all of those years? Did it mean I couldn't work through my path of grief and still find the blessings in the legacy I carried? I realized this was the journey to healing.

What about *you*? What are you carrying in your own life? What legacy are you creating for yourself and those you influence and impact? Is the load you bring forward one of learning lessons, truth, joy, and a walk of legacy you want others to know? Where are you trusting and leaning into your faith and God's truth? As scripture tells us, "He will never leave us nor forsake us." That is our constant, where belief will grow. Yes, the stories of family remain. They were our foundation in many ways, even if they are filled with "dysfunction" and challenges, we started there… we chose to grow from there… to where we are now.

Are you aware that in our baptism experience, the pastor immerses us in the water just like John the Baptist performed for many, including Jesus? Then, the pastor raises us up through the water and says, "Arise IN HIM." Have you ever thought about that phrase? Arise IN HIM. Raise up IN HIM. You were born anew IN HIM. Powerful words! You already have everything you need IN HIM. YOU are now part of the family; the sisters, brothers, and more IN Christ. The legacy connection has been made. Welcome!

Now, we embrace *belonging* and *legacy* in Him.

Many times as humans, even in Biblical times, we sabotage our own understanding of being *in* legacy already. Author Steven Pressfield writes about how resistance is the most dangerous aspect of the dreams and visions the Lord instills within us. The hopes of life IN HIM are derailed by fears, anxiety, distractions, and doubt, which we know are tools of the enemy in our own lives. That is where we only see lack—not love and legacy. How do we see through these obstacles and challenges that arise? We ground ourselves again "IN HIM" and in the legacies He left for us to follow through His word. Realizing we are all part of the family of the Lord is powerful. Rising up in Jesus, united in His name, we are now more than conquerors. That is the "living legacy" we carry and have that innate desire to share with others.

How do you walk forward with *ease* and *grace* in the Lord when you are carrying things that serve only *you* and not the Lord? His burden is light—when we accept it. Each step in our journey and calling with the Lord matters, and it is to be honored. Even in loss, even in burdens placed on us like familiar fear, trauma, guilt, shame, or secrets. When we decide to lighten the load and choose to honor the *legacy* in the Lord, we let go of the childish things. We hold fast to honoring the love and restoration of our lives and break the generational binds for us and for the next ages to come. As we bring forth the Kingdom of God onto the earth, we have assignments to carry as we

> "When we accept and receive the Lord's legacy, we elevate in His name."
>
> *lori l. dixon*

complete our legacies.

As Nehemiah shared with his people, "This day is sacred to our Lord. Do not grieve, for the joy of the Lord is your strength" (Nehemiah 8:10, NKJV). When we release the loss and longing of this earth, which has created the numbness and fear of walking forward, the heavier burdens we carry—we can RISE. When we accept and receive the Lord's legacy, we elevate in His name. He takes our burdens and gives us joy and we *rise* in Him.

As we rise, we feel the urging to write, speak, and share our own testimonies of our legacy in Him. At this time, many are finding and accepting the new understanding of who Christ is. The next step is for us who have carried pieces of the legacy in Him—our purpose—for new Christians to grow further and find their own next steps for the Lord.

Yes, we have been led by the Lord to create spaces for others to *rise* in the Legacy of the Lord. That is how our community, authors, speakers, entrepreneurs, and more have been launched through the WoW programs and offerings. We believe in enhancing the Wisdom on the Walk you receive from God and through His Word.

Receiving His legacy is already within you. Will you accept it? Will you honor it?

Reflection

Where do you believe your legacy in life lies? How will you nurture and grow in it so you are growing IN Him?

The journey of faith is a narrow road. How is that evident in your own life and how would you describe your path?

Where do you need to shift from lack and loss to legacy and love? Identity those areas that may even be deeply embedded within you.

_____

_____

_____

_____

_____

_____

_____

_____

_____

_____

_____

_____

_____

_____

_____

Prayer to God

Dear Lord,

I lift up this person reading the words of legacy today. Let them know how loved and treasured they truly are and how deep their legacy and importance is in our Lord. I ask that they know You even more deeply, feel Your presence even stronger, and walk with You even more directed by Your Word in their life. May they be able to embrace You and Your truth and release the lack that has been felt and instilled within them.

Eradicate the feeling of not good enough, not worthy, not faithful enough... not enough. Bring forth Your loving arms and meet them where they are, right now, on the journey You have placed them on today. Let them know You are walking with them in all they do.

We love and honor You today, Lord. Thank you for being in our lives and in every breath we take.

Amen.

deepening your walk

Scripture Verse

"And now, because we are united in Christ, we both have equal and direct access in the realm of the Holy Spirit to come before the Father. So, you are not foreigners or guests, but rather you are the children of the city of the holy ones, with all the rights as family members of the household of God. You are rising like the perfectly fitted stones of the temple and your lives have been built up together upon the foundation laid by the apostles and prophets, and best of all, you are connected to the Head Cornerstone of the building, the Anointed One, Jesus Christ himself."

Ephesians 2:18-20 (TPT)

Translations

Key Words

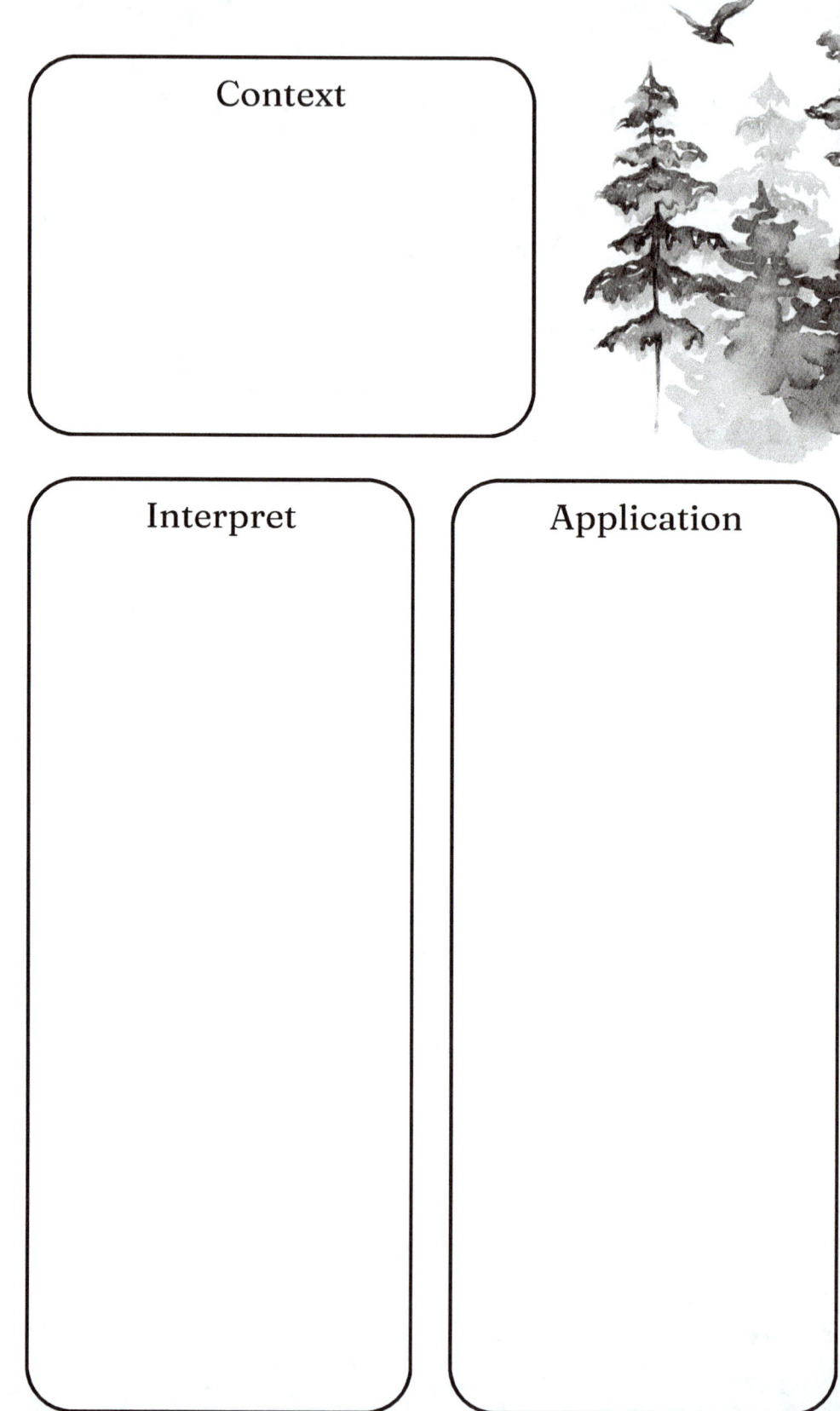

Context

Interpret

Application

steadfast

Niki Banning

> Because your steadfast love is better than life, my lips will praise you. So I will bless you as long as I live; in your name I will lift up my hands.
>
> Psalm 63:3-4 (ESV)

> Our identity rests in God's relentless tenderness for us revealed in Jesus Christ.
>
> *Brennan Manning*

Growing up, I spent summers in southern Missouri, running around the grounds of my grandparents' camp, Arcadia Valley Bible Camp. My cousins went to camp with me and were some of my best friends all those summers. Camp-wide chapel, with morning and evening services, were the foundation to our experience each year. Chapel was a beautiful time of singing songs, both the silly and then the move-you-to-tears kind. There were amusing skits and serious sermons about Jesus. Altar calls and prayers, lives changed forever.

I remember doing crafts with my cabin mates, playing camp-wide games, swimming in the "creek," and making campers run around the mess hall when we caught each other with elbows on the table during meals. Choruses of "Round the Mess Hall you must go, you must go, you must go!" were to be avoided at all costs—but inevitably rang out at each mealtime. Shenanigans and pranks by both campers and counselors were on the agenda daily.

The smell of my grandma's homemade rolls would deliciously fill the camp, beckoning us to the Mess Hall for a delightful meal, cooked with lots of love by strong, capable hands. Homemade donuts, cooked by those same hands, awaited us many mornings. Even from a young age, I remember being in awe of Grandma's cooking skills, amazed how she could bake effortlessly—and with so much care—for 100 or more campers at a time.

Our counselors prayed with and for us each day. Toward the end of each week of camp, each camper and counselor, along with every leader, would trek through the woods to the roaring bonfire, gather under blankets, sing our favorite worship songs, and earnestly listen as campers shared their testimonies. Heartstring-pulling stories shared about how they came to know the Lord as their Savior and how He touched their lives. I so admired the kids who had the courage to get up and share.

And then there was the summer that's forever soul-seared; locked in the most sacred space of my heart. The summer I asked Jesus into my heart. I was 10 years old and having the time of my life at camp. As we left our evening chapel session, I remember the muggy summer air on my face—and the tears that wouldn't stop rolling down my cheeks. I knew something had to change. Not later, but right then. I felt the gentle, persistent tug from His heart, urging me to follow Him. The weight of the message gripped my heart.

One of my older cousins, a boys' counselor that summer, stopped me and asked why I was crying. Honestly, I wasn't completely sure. But I knew Jesus was speaking to my heart, calling me to Himself. Then and there, on the big rocks beside the creek, my cousin walked me through the Prayer of Salvation. I realized I was a sinner, separated from God, and asked Him to come into my heart and be my Savior.

Camp was a huge influence on my Christian life, and between those wonderful summers, I regularly attended church. We attended Sunday morning services, sitting together as a family. I remember the feeling of my mom's soft hand in mine as we sang hymns and worship songs. If there were Sunday evening services, we were there. I even went to Awana on Wednesdays, hanging out with other young believers, memorizing scripture and learning Bible stories.

You see, in all my life circles, I was completely surrounded by faith-filled folks who encouraged me to seek the Lord with my whole heart. My mom, a beacon of strength for our family, radiated His love for my siblings and me—even through her most challenging and upended times. I saw the church body being the hands and feet of Jesus to our family through their tangible care for Mom and our family. God was present and evident all around me for as long as I can remember.

And so—I *knew* Jesus loved me (the Bible tells me so!). I *knew* He was my Light and my Salvation. I knew beyond a shadow of a doubt that I was changed forever that summer night at Arcadia Valley Bible Camp.

I was saved.

But still—a piece was... missing. Many years and many struggles later, I would understand that I had allowed my identity to be found in nearly anything but Jesus.

> A new command I give you: Love each other. As I have loved you, so you must love one another. By this everyone will know that you are my disciples, if you love one another.
>
> John 13:34-35 (NIV)

My dad left our family when I was eight years old. That day is forever etched in my heart, the memories clear. I was called out of my second-grade classroom to meet Dad in the office. As I walked the forever-long hall to the office, I remember looking at the artwork from other classrooms, hanging crookedly on the walls as I passed. My mind wandered, confused as to why my dad might need to have me called out of class. I stepped over brown and black marbled tiles, considering what might be happening.

The entirety of the conversation that took place on those big concrete steps in front of my school building is a bit of a blur. But one thing was certain. Dad was leaving—and that was that. I was left feeling completely disoriented. My young mind couldn't quite comprehend the depth and full impact of what my dad told me that day. I recall being angry and very confused—but mostly unsure what I could have possibly done to make my dad want to leave our family.

My three siblings, my mom, and I were left to navigate the broken and winding trail without Dad's presence. His absence left a hole in our little family and most certainly in my young heart. It was a God-sized hole that I would not allow to be filled with Him for years to come.

Unanswered questions plagued me and left a residual feeling of unworthiness in my heart. And, although subconsciously, I allowed doubt and uncertainty to plant a wall between me and my Heavenly Father.

> "Oh, that I had only understood how much my Heavenly Father loved me. And how His heart broke for the pain and hurt I felt."
>
> *niki banning*

How could I trust the Lord if I couldn't trust my earthly father to care for, love, and protect my family and me? The thought of feeling "close" to God was not an option to my little heart. He felt a million miles away. My whole world had been shaken.

Oh, that I had only understood how much my Heavenly Father loved me—and how His heart broke for the pain and hurt I felt.

I felt lost.

But Psalm 27:10 (NIV) reminded me, "Though my father and mother forsake me, the Lord will receive me."

In middle school, anorexia came into my life like a whirlwind. Careless words from friends coupled with insecurities around boys came together in a perfect storm, unleashing deeply-held thoughts of inadequacy and self-doubt about myself.

I hid my disorder well until my sophomore year in high school—when there could no longer be a denial of what was happening. The full weight of the disease wrecked my body and any athletic aspirations I might have had. There were neurological tests, confirming the progression of muscular tissue damage. There were fears for my recovery if I continued down the path. I could no longer participate in track or volleyball until I began to take care of my body and mind, and healing began to take place. More than twelve months of physical activity were taken away with the stroke of a physician's pen. I felt I had lost my identity yet again.

But the most profound consequence of all—anorexia dug a deeper hole into my heart and soul. The spiral of "not enoughness" swirled furiously around me. I felt like a complete failure, both physically and emotionally. I had let my mom and coaches down. I let myself down. Counseling and even hospitalization followed. I could not understand the "why" of what had happened. Why had I taken myself down this self-inflicted path of pain? How could this happen?

I remember feeling as though I wasn't and would never be enough; not pretty enough, smart enough, funny enough—simply not enough. Yet another empty space in my heart, yearning to be filled. It was a battle I would fight for many years to come.

And I wondered. How could a great big God *like* me, let alone look at me with love as His own beloved child?

I was hurting. I felt unseen and alone.

> The Lord is near to the brokenhearted and saves those who are crushed in spirit.
>
> Psalm 34:18 (NIV)

Still unaware of my Heavenly Father's vast and unchanging love for me—and quite unsure of who I was as I marched into adulthood, I found myself navigating through failed relationships and marriages.

Anorexia and insecurity continued to follow me,

unwelcome guests on my journey. Self-doubt and searching were constant companions.

Through divorce, custody challenges, through all the heartaches, pains, and disappointments—I felt alone and unworthy—and sought my identity in all the wrong places.

But God, in His infinite grace, mercy, and love, pursued me relentlessly. He never stopped. Through the pain, the choices that took me off His path, through the doubts, fears, and uncertainty—He was always there.

I didn't know His steady, ever-guiding, and always-compassionate hand had always been with me, holding me, watching over me each step of the way.

"But God, in His infinite grace, mercy, and love, pursued me relentlessly. He never stopped."

niki banning

I could see His blessings through each of my kiddos; from the oldest to the youngest, they were His love personified in my life. They were an ever-present reminder of His goodness to me, even on days when life's problems seemed insurmountable.

Family members and dear friends stood behind, supporting and surrounding me in prayer, even when I wasn't aware.

I was held.

> For I, the Lord your God, hold your right hand; it is I who says to you, "Fear not, I am the one who helps you."
>
> Isaiah 41:13 (ESV)

Fast forward a few years.

I continued to dig more deeply into the "whys" of my choices and allowed self-awareness and spiritual growth to be part of my daily life. And while seeking the Lord through scripture, prayer, and seeking His heart for my identity—life-changing revelations began to pour over me. A lifeline, straight from His heart to mine. They pierced my very soul.

In the most unexpected ways, God began to reveal Himself to me. Beautifully and gently. Slowly, the God-sized hole began to be filled with knowledge of Him and His steadfast love over me. I began reading my Bible like never before. It wasn't a "have to," it was a desire, a hunger for His Word. A desire to learn more about Jesus, to soak up stories of His life and ministry. To understand God's character and who He truly is. To know the Holy Spirit more intimately and discern His voice in my life.

"He gently responded, 'Lift up your head. *Keep your eyes on Me.* I created you. I am the One who fills the holes in your heart. *I love you.*'"

niki banning

After one spectacularly failed relationship, I remember falling to my knees, asking God, "Why? Why do I keep doing this? What is wrong with me?"

He gently responded, "Lift up your head. *Keep your eyes on Me.* I created you. I am the One who fills the holes in your heart. *I love you.*"

I'd love to say understanding and acceptance completely sank in that day. But they didn't. What happened, however, was the beginning of bigger steps toward healing and a receiving of His steadfast love over me. The God-sized holes began to be filled by their rightful Owner. My heart was finally beginning to open to Him.

By no coincidence or accident (God sure has His ways, doesn't He?), I joined *Becoming a Legacy Builder*, a Biblical Money Mindset Coaching group, led by a remarkable Christian entrepreneur, Charissa Quade.

After wrestling out the decision with God, I finally took the leap of faith. I had fears and doubts about joining Charissa's program, but God clearly asked me to trust Him in walking this path. He didn't just want me to be a woman of faith; He required fully trusting in and relying on Him as my source.

Upon joining Charissa's group, I had expectations of insight with my business and life financial goals, plans, and dreams. But God, in His infinite, all-knowing ways, had so much more in store for me than I ever could have imagined. As I launched excitedly into Charissa's teachings, I discovered the very first lesson was around *Identity*. Hmmm. While I wasn't sure what identity had to do with my financial life and mindset, I was open to learning and growing in this area where I certainly felt "less-than."

Even now, as I look back over the hand-scribbled notes from this lesson, I am moved to tears. All at once—God broke through.

Biblical truths are embedded into Charissa's program, and she encouraged us to delve deeply into scriptures as we worked through our money mindset issues. And God, in His ever-knowing and unfathomably loving ways, gave me a scripture that would *finally* allow me to see Him for the Daddy He is and wants to be to *me*.

Isaiah 30:18 (NIV) leapt off the page and spoke directly to my heart: "Yet the LORD longs to be gracious to you; therefore he will rise up to show you compassion. For the

Lord is a God of justice. Blessed are all who wait for him!"

I read that verse time and again. And it changed me. I could feel His heart for me.

He *longs* to be gracious to me (and you!). He will rise up to show me (and you!) compassion. Wow. I was reduced to tears that, once again, wouldn't stop. He LONGS to be gracious to me (and you!). The phrase played over and over in my mind, soaking into my soul. I embraced this thought, allowing His compassionate love to pour over me. It felt like a warm blanket, soothing and healing my aching soul. My heart fully received the understanding that He looks at me with love as the child He created with intentionality. With His steadfast love.

As my love of reading the Bible grew, I began to receive Holy Spirit downloads—little God-sized nuggets of understanding and insight—like never before. Bible stories I'd learned as a child took on whole new meaning. The depth and richness of The Word was astounding.

As I continued to read my Bible, asking God to reveal more of Himself every day—I was astonished to see how many times the word "steadfast" was used to describe God and His amazing love for us.

It's spoken close to 200 times, as a matter of fact. The Book of Psalms alone contains 196 of the 200 times "steadfast" is used. Remarkable. I highlighted as I read, wondering why in the world I hadn't seen it before. God continued to peel back the layers of my identity with each "steadfast" I read, revealing His truth to me.

| But the steadfast love of the Lord is from everlasting to

> everlasting on those who fear him, and his righteousness to children's children, to those who keep his covenant and remember to do his commandments.
>
> Psalm 103:17-18 (ESV)

> When I thought, "My foot slips," your steadfast love, O Lord, held me up.
>
> Psalm 94:18 (ESV)

My identity is only found in Him.

He is Steadfast. His love for me is unchanging, anchored, and never-ending.

I am chosen. I am His. I am steadfastly loved.

> The steadfast love of the Lord never ceases; his mercies never come to an end; they are new every morning; great is your faithfulness.
>
> Lamentations 3:22-23 (ESV)

As God shared more of His heart with me, my heart began to shift. I could release my dad in forgiveness and walk more deeply into healing. I could release the burden of expectations placed on others; time spent looking to anyone other than God to fill those empty spaces in me.

Hemmed in by His steadfast love, I have recognized and released my fears of not being enough. I have let go of feeling alone, of not feeling protected or cared for by Him or my earthly father. God has faithfully shown up in my life, from my early years at camp all the way through today. His love is steadfast and unchanging.

Looking back, I see clearly how God has continually sat me at tables with those who surrounded me, lifted me up, and pointed me back to Him. He lovingly and knowingly placed friends, family, counselors, and leaders in camp before I ever experienced my dad leaving—so I could be surrounded by love and guiding hands in the absence of my father.

He showed up in middle and high school, even when I was subconsciously determined to agree with what I believed others were showing me—that I was not enough to love and take care of. Not worthy of who He created me to be. His hand was with me through every appointment, every doubt, every fear, and through steps to recovery.

He was there through failed relationships, sustaining me and reminding me "Lift up your head. *Keep your eyes on Me.* I created you. I am the One who fills the holes in your heart. *I love you.*" (With an unending, steadfast love!)

Even now, His steadfast love is very real and present, embracing and surrounding me in the everyday moments of life. He shows up still today through my relationships, my business—and most especially, in my quiet times of sitting with Him and His precious and living Word.

Never once has He left my side. He is Steadfast.

And I am His.

Reflection

Words and actions can hurt. Can you recall a time when you were hurt deeply by someone's words or actions? What did you do with that pain?

Decisions in life can keep us aligned with God's heart for us or take us off-track. Have you ever made a choice that took you away from Him? How did you find your way back?

Life can catch us up in the whirlwind of experiences around us, and it's easy to forget that God is not *in the chaos. He is* our God of peace, details, intentional *love, and steadfast hope.* Where have you seen God's steadfast love in your life? What transformation has His steadfastness brought to you?

Prayer to God

Father God, thank You for Your never-changing, ever-abiding, steadfast love. You are our hope, our shield, and our place of refuge.

Lord, I ask that You show my sweet sister how much You love her, just as she is. Just how You created her to be. She was created by You with intention, and she is carried by Your steadfast love.

Through Your great love, help her release feelings of being alone, of being too much or not enough, to let go of feelings of unworthiness. Show her how much she is valued, Father. How much You desire to protect and care for her.

May she come to know you as Abba Father, her Daddy, the One she can run to in times of struggle. May she know Your voice and feel Your very real peace in her life.

Holy Spirit, speak gentle words of encouragement to her soul. Uplift and guide her daily. Jesus, heal any spaces in her heart that need You. Father, may she learn to see herself as You see her. Fearfully, wonderfully, uniquely made. And steadfastly loved.

In Your Precious and Holy Name,

Amen.

deepening your walk

Scripture Verse

"Yet the Lord longs to be gracious to you; therefore he will rise up to show you compassion. For the Lord is a God of justice. Blessed are all who wait for him!"

Isaiah 30:18 (NIV)

Translations

Key Words

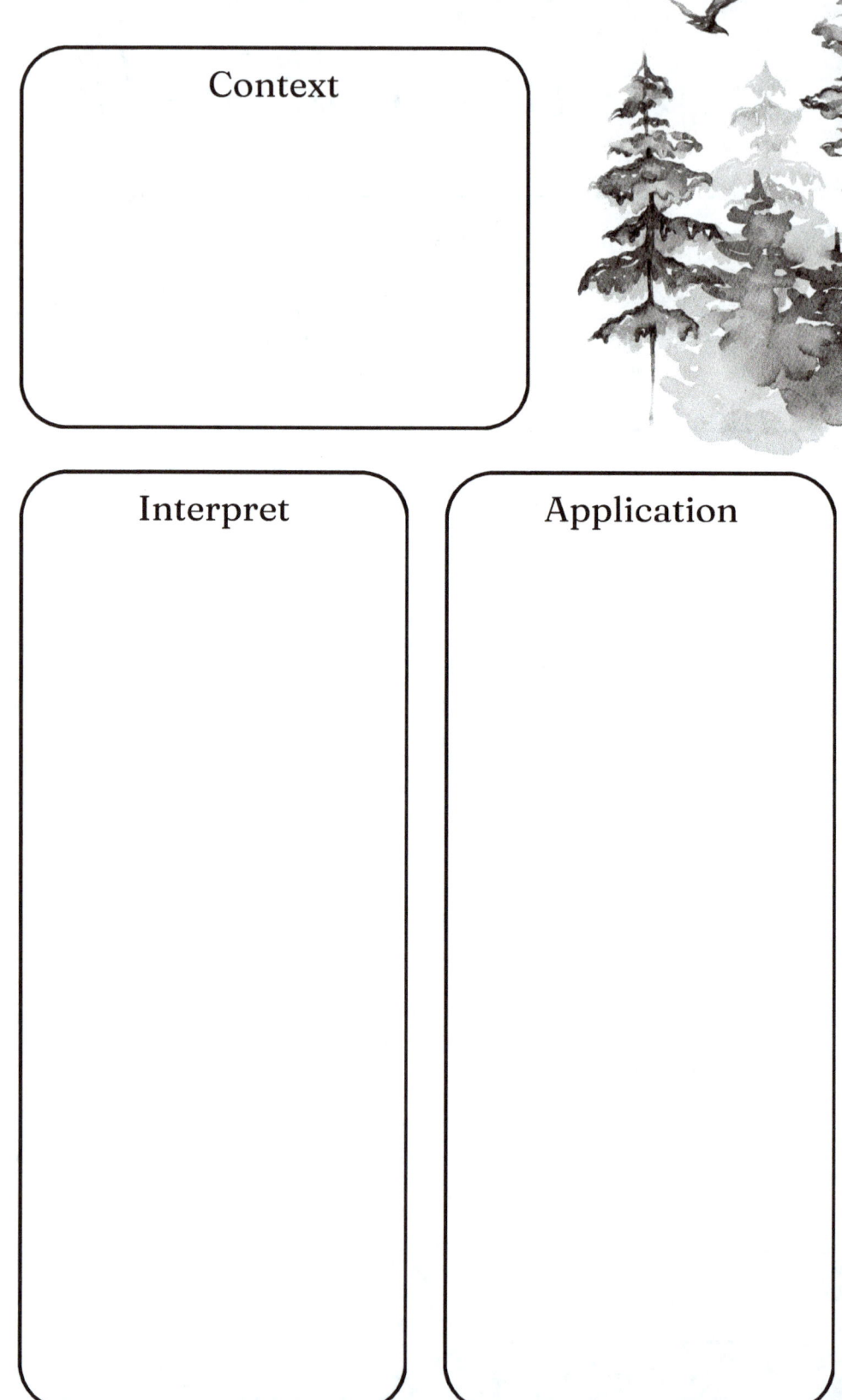

Context

Interpret

Application

not just another prodigal story

Natalie Merrill

I praise you, for I am fearfully and wonderfully made.

Psalm 139:14 (ESV)

Do you know how important you are? Do you know that Satan, the enemy, is tirelessly pursuing your soul? But Jesus loves you so much He died for you, so your soul can live in Him forever? It doesn't matter what color, what disability, what physical disposition you were born with, what race, what country, what financial standing you are in—no matter what you have done, no matter what has been done to you—you were made in God's image.

You are God's beautiful creation!

You can find the parable of the lost son in Luke 15:11-32 (NKJV). This passage talks about a wealthy father who has two sons. The younger son wanted the wealth that was due to him before his father passed away. His father agreed and gave it to the son. He became independent from his father and squandered the wealth on his own values and wants. The son spent all the money on worthless things and was in a terrible place. He came to himself and decided to go back to his father and ask for forgiveness. The father forgave him, welcomed his son with open arms, and celebrated his return.

For many years, I thought I knew what the prodigal parable meant, but I wondered if I was a prodigal. One day, I saw a pamphlet in church saying that a prodigal is a child who has turned away from their parents' religious beliefs. I thought yes, that was me. I was a prodigal. You see, when I became a teenager, I decided to be independent. I didn't want to believe in my parents' religion. I ran away. Actually, I ran away a couple of times. I wanted to make my own choices, to be free from the many restrictions. I wanted to find out what I was made for. But—unlike the prodigal son, what inheritance did I have to squander? My parents didn't give me an inheritance. Or did they?

This chapter is about my prodigal story and healing journey. I have been blessed to be a part of some amazing groups with wonderful resources. These groups have helped me not only see my own sins, but helped me begin to recognize generational sins in my life. I have learned how to forgive others and how to forgive myself. I have also learned the importance of having healthy boundaries.

Growing up, my parents were missionaries. I was born in London, England. Much of my youth was spent in South America. I lived in Chile for a while, but later predominantly lived in Uruguay. From my teen to adult years, I lived in Southern California. You could say I was a naïve missionary kid.

> Train up a child in the way he should go [teaching him to seek God's wisdom and will for his abilities and talents], Even when he is old he will not depart from it.
>
> Proverbs 22:6 (AMP)

The most important thing my parents ever did was introduce me to Jesus. Because of my early introduction to the Lord, I developed a personal relationship with Jesus over the years. Growing up, my true desire was to shine my light—the light God gave me to share with others. However, I was very aware of my daily sins, which made it difficult to shine my light. I believed everyone else was more important than me. I knew I was God's creation, but I never felt beautiful or worthy. Feeling this way led me to make some wrong decisions throughout my life.

I knew God created us in His image and His breath gave our original bloodline life through a man named Adam. Then, the enemy of our souls showed up with temptation and a little bit of truth to taint the perfect bloodline we were born into. Adam and Eve, our bloodline, were cast away from the home we were meant for. They were given the deceptive option of the knowledge of good and evil and the option to be dependent or independent from God. To this day, we all have the choice of evil and death or love and life. Among my choices—I became a prodigal.

So, what happened? Why did I turn away from my parents' religious beliefs? That was never my plan. I've come to realize it had a lot to do with my reaction to things that were going on around me and my own tainted generational sin nature. Many people believe I must have been blessed most of my life because I was introduced to Jesus at an early age. When people ask me what it was like being a missionary child, I simply tell them it was very character-building.

> And yet, O Lord, you are our Father. We are the clay, and you are the potter. We all are formed by your hand. Don't be angry with us, Lord. Please don't remember our sin forever. Look at us, we pray and see that we are all your people.
>
> Isaiah 64:8-9 (NLT)

I am a sinner saved by grace.

Facing traumas in my life has been a struggle, but learning about generational sin has helped me recognize the sins that have been embedded in me, passed down through generations. Our family bloodline is tainted by external and internal factors. Growing up, there were so many things that were confusing about religion, people, and the world.

My confusion started when I was five years old. I was sexually traumatized by people I thought were believers. But even then, at the tender young age of five, I knew that God was with me. I felt the Holy Spirit comfort me that night. His Spirit was like a warm wave that flowed over me from head to toe, letting me know everything was going to be okay and that He had a purpose for even this.

Throughout my life, there was an emphasis on being pure, which is what I wanted—even as a teenager. However, no matter how much I wanted to be pure, I knew that precious purity had been taken away. I looked for love and acceptance from other people in all the wrong ways, independent from God.

Due to traveling with my missionary family and being in many different educational situations, school was a constant struggle throughout my childhood. I was bullied verbally and physically while in different countries, both by the wealthy kids who were in my school and by other missionary kids we lived with. I was extremely behind by the time I got to junior high and was continually sent to the computer lab to try and "catch up."

I wanted to be around other kids who were believers and get involved in fun events with a positive community. Yet, I went to a high school that was an hour away which hindered my ability to socialize and my involvement in sports. I felt like an outsider much of the time.

I remember someone asking me, "What is wrong with you? You seem intelligent." In my mind I thought, "I wish I knew—can you tell me what is wrong with me? I feel so worthless. Can you tell me how I can make all this better? Can you help me be normal? I feel like an alien." Most of my life, I believed I was the "stupid girl." I carried the titles that people gave me. And I struggled with the expectations people had for me. I would try to live up to their expectations, but I would always fall short.

Inside I was crying out, but no one could hear me. I would pray, speak to Jesus, and trust that eventually He would show me a purpose for it all. The Holy Spirit did give me peace, and I knew Jesus was there.

I remember a time I was alone on the playground, swinging and looking up in the sky, feeling the wind on my face. I felt peace, and longed for the time I would be in heaven with Jesus. I looked forward to being in heaven, knowing there would be a time when I would never feel emptiness, pain, or sorrow again.

Have you ever felt that way? When you hear someone make a statement about you and your self-talk doesn't match who you really are, it is hard to see the good—and all you hear is bad?

When you felt that way, did you seek Jesus and allow

His arms to be your refuge? Did He nurture and guide you in those times?

Growing up as a missionary kid was challenging. The missionary organization my parents belonged to barely gave my parents enough money to survive in a foreign country. The financial strain caused arguments over even the smallest of things. One time, I remember my mom yelling at my dad because he bought me a coloring book and crayons. I was aware we were sacrificing to introduce people to Jesus, and I was expected to adapt. And I did. But while adapting, it seemed to me that Jesus came to save everyone else but me. I thought Jesus was always watching and judging me, making sure I was doing everything right. In my reaction, I did a lot of things that were wrong. No matter how hard I tried on my own to do everything right, I couldn't do it on my own.

In Romans, the Bible tells us that even Paul couldn't do everything right on his own either:

> But if I do what I don't want to do, I am not really the one doing wrong; it is sin living in me that does it. I have discovered this principle of life—that when I want to do what is right, I inevitably do what is wrong. I love God's law with all my heart. But there is another power within me that is at war with my mind. This power makes me a slave to the sin that is still within me.
>
> Romans 7:20-23 (NLT)

I've learned that generational depression and fear run in my mom's side of the family. Looking back, I realized my mom was sad and depressed quite often, which rarely left time for her to think about other things. It seldom seemed like my mom had time for me. It appeared that she was consumed with her own insecurities. It was very evident that my mom wasn't secure in the countries where we lived. I not only remember my parents arguing about money, but I also remember my mom having trouble with the languages and trouble fitting in. My dad did not understand the emotional turmoil my mom was experiencing. Instead, Dad would yell back, with lack of compassion or understanding for what my mom was going through. After one of their arguments, I remember going to my mom and hugging her, telling her God would provide.

When my mom did have time for me, I didn't know how to tell her what was going on in my world. I believed it would just add to what she was going through. It didn't seem like she knew how to get through her challenges, so how would she be able to help me? It was a difficult lesson to learn as a child. However, I knew Jesus, my friend, was with me through it all.

Generational anger came from my dad's side of the family. When I was punished, I learned to stuff my feelings inward. I believe my dad was going through his own internal triggers while he was punishing me. His own frustrations were released on me as I was being punished. As my dad punished me, he would tell me not to cry; if I cried it would be worse. So, to this day—I stuff my feelings.

Proverbs 13:24 (NLT) tells us, "Those who spare the rod of discipline hate their children. Those who love their children care enough to discipline them."

I believe many parents misunderstand this scripture and punish the only way they know how. In their own way—they are showing their children their love.

The following scripture was brought to my attention at a very young age. It is the fifth commandment:

> "Honor your father and mother." This is the first commandment with a promise: if you honor your father and mother, things will go well for you, and you will have a long life on the earth.
>
> Ephesians 6:2-3 (NLT)

While it is a commandment to honor your father and mother, I don't believe it means to punish or persuade your child into honoring you. The scripture goes on to say, "Fathers, do not exasperate your children; instead, bring them up in the training and instruction of the Lord" (Ephesians 6:4, NIV).

I do not believe the Lord disciplines us the way my dad was disciplined as a child—or the way my dad disciplined me. That was a harsh realization for me. Now that I have a daughter of my own, I keep the following scripture in mind: "Understand this, my dear brothers and sisters: You must all be quick to listen, slow to speak, and slow to get angry. Human anger does not produce the righteousness God desires" (James 1:19-20, NLT). I know when my daughter is making bad decisions, there are other factors involved. And I want her to be able to talk to me about what is going on in her world—without fear.

> For all have sinned and fall short of the glory of God.
>
> Romans 3:23 (NIV)

Parenting is to be done in love, showing the way of the Lord and His Word, guiding and modifying behavior through understanding. Instead, what can occur through generational and imposed sin is shame and other triggers that are not ours to carry. These are strongholds and sins that we did not choose, yet they have a tremendous impact on the growth in our identity and mental well-being.

Forgiveness. What does it look like to forgive others? What does it look like to forgive ourselves? It took me years to really grasp that I was truly forgiven and accept God's forgiveness. I was tainted by the enemy's bloodline. The enemy is a liar. He will give us a little truth to try and get us to stray away from knowing who we really are meant to be in Christ. The Lord does not create the bad things that have happened to us; we are affected by the sins of other people, just as they are affected by our sins.

When I was sexually traumatized as a child, I was punished as though I was the culprit—even though I was the victim by someone that wasn't even part of my family. The imposed sin that was forced on me was traumatic. It caused me to have triggers and reactions I have struggled to learn to control, even into adulthood.

The shame, imposed by the enemy, can twist everything that has happened in our lives and point at it as being our own fault. When in fact, it is not mine or yours to carry or repent for.

How do we forgive others when we know what they did was wrong? So many things that happen seem like they should be unforgivable. However, when we don't forgive, the enemy of our souls keeps us in bondage, unable to accept or give God's grace.

What is important to remember is Jesus died for all those sins and through His perfect, pure blood, His bloodline, we are able to be cleansed from all sin so we can be with Him. I needed to let go and accept the pure blood of Jesus—His perfect, untainted

"I am meant for a perfect bloodline. And you are meant for a perfect bloodline."

natalie merrill

blood. I am meant for a perfect bloodline. And you are meant for a perfect bloodline.

Even now, I ask God daily to forgive me for not believing and trusting Him. I know I am His masterpiece, and He created me for a reason. The enemy of our souls continues to seek who he can destroy. I realize that when I try to do things in my own strength, independent from God. That is when I really get myself in trouble. Don't you? It is truly so much more fulfilling and comfortable when we are in His arms, navigated by His desires for us.

In a weakened time of my life, I was walking independently from God—as a prodigal. I turned to drugs to numb the pain and emptiness of my life. After much self-reflection, I realized that, even then, I knew I was broken. I knew I needed something, someone. It was my way of being able to fit in with this world. There was a point where I didn't feel anything. I was in turmoil. I got on my hands and knees, begging God to let me feel again. That step became my desire; to shift from things and people of the world to those of the Lord—where truth, grace, and healing reside.

I was beginning to heal. The next step was to again ask Jesus to forgive me for my sin. But I realized I was still holding onto my shame. I was not able to forgive myself. I asked Jesus to show me my sins—those I knew of and those I wasn't even unaware of.

Healing was now in progress. I had never voluntarily fasted, but Jesus put me on a fast for three days. It was an immensely difficult process, but I felt it was necessary. On the third evening, I had a dream where all my sins flooded me. I was crying out, I felt I deserved the pain. I deserve this emptiness, this worthlessness. Then Jesus was there beside me and He said to me, "That is what I forgave you for. I forgave you for those sins. Why do you want to carry them with you? Why do you want to be apart from Me?

You need to make a choice! Do you want to choose your sin or Me?" In my dream, I said, "I choose you, Jesus! I choose You!" It was a powerful transition in my life.

As you go on your healing journey, it is important to remember to forgive yourself and forgive others. And understand the shame isn't yours to carry. Ask God to show you the sins that need repentance, then accept his forgiveness, choosing Jesus.

To be forgiven, we need to know what true forgiveness means. Forgive those people and circumstances that were out of your control—generational and imposed sins. Those were never yours to carry. What was done to you may have been wrong. You were sinned against. You were put in situations where you had no dignity. You were violated, betrayed, shamed, and blamed.

However, if you keep carrying that with you, you will not find peace. You will not be able to have a right relationship with God. You will not feel the Lord's presence; you may even feel empty, as I did. I had to realize and accept that I must forgive and acknowledge I am not fighting those people—I am rejecting the enemy. Now, it is your turn.

We all have a choice.

> For we are not fighting against flesh-and-blood enemies, but against evil rulers and authorities of the unseen world, against mighty powers in this dark world, and against evil spirits in the heavenly places.
>
> Ephesians 6:12-18 (NLT)

I choose Jesus every day, reminding myself I can't forgive or live the way I am meant to without giving it all to Him, allowing Jesus to live and work through me.

Jesus died for you. He died for the sins of all people.

He died for your sin. The blood of Jesus is pure. You may even look at it as your blood being tainted by generational strongholds, but Jesus shed His blood so that if you ask God for forgiveness and you believe that Jesus died for you, you will be saved. He died to cleanse you of all of those sins with His perfect blood. And when you accept Him, you become a new creation. You have hope. You see how you are fearfully and wonderfully made. You have a purpose. You have a Loving Father, a Loving Brother, a Friend who is with you, protecting you wherever you go.

> "You have a purpose. You have a Loving Father, a Loving Brother, a Friend who is with you, protecting you wherever you go."
>
> *natalie merrill*

When I was younger, I was disillusioned by the enemy to believe that to honor God meant allowing people to do whatever they wanted so I would live up to their expectations. Now I know that simply isn't true. Honoring God requires the Lord's boundaries within us.

Now when someone tries to tell me who I am or what I should do, I remember who I am in Christ. It is also important for me to have boundaries in my own mind and follow His path and purpose for me. I remind myself who I am in Jesus, in His body. I am part of the body of Christ. I don't have to let people shame me, hurt me, or mistreat me. In Jesus, life looks much different, because I know who I am in Christ. I can release the hold that those people, those traumas, had on me—and know my true identity. I can live the way I was meant to live.

Often in my youth, when I was around religious believers and leaders, they would emphasize how to study the Bible. When I didn't study the Bible like they did, I felt like they were telling me there is this amazing God and Heavenly Realm I couldn't possibly reach, because I wasn't studying the right way. So, most of my life I prayed, and I just talked to Jesus. That was my way of having a relationship with Jesus. Do you know you can talk to Jesus whenever you want to, even if it is simply in your thoughts?

Now when I read the Bible, it is spending time with Jesus. It is part of having a relationship with Him. The Bible is the Living Word. It is the Sword of the Spirit.

These scriptures capture how I defend myself now:

> Therefore, put on every piece of God's armor so you will be able to resist the enemy in the time of evil. Then after the battle you will still be standing firm. Stand your ground, putting on the belt of truth and the body armor of God's righteousness. For shoes, put on the peace that comes from the Good News so that you will be fully prepared. In addition to all of these, hold up the shield of faith to stop the fiery arrows of the devil. Put on salvation as your helmet, and take the sword of the Spirit, which is the word of God. Pray in the Spirit at all times and on every occasion. Stay alert and be persistent in your prayers for all believers everywhere.
>
> Ephesians 6:12-18 (NLT)

So, was I a prodigal? Yes, I was. And sometimes, I still lose sight of choosing Jesus and His love. Choosing life. However, I don't believe I was a prodigal simply because I turned away from my parents' religion. I was a prodigal because I turned away from the bloodline I was created to carry.

Through the healing process, I faced traumas, fears, and anger. I have faced and acknowledged generational sin. I have gone through the forgiving process by forgiving others and myself, and I have learned how to have healthy

> "He welcomes me back with celebration, into His Loving arms, every time."
>
> *natalie merrill*

boundaries. It has been hard—because it is hard.

I shut down so many times writing this chapter; it was my defensive reaction to facing these experiences. However, writing and facing what we don't want to face with Jesus and the Holy Spirit is what it takes to heal. It is what it takes to truly be the new creation we were meant to be.

I became a prodigal because I turned away from my Father God. But you know what? He welcomes me back with celebration, into His Loving arms, every time.

Reflection

What situation, possibly even from childhood, has brought confusion into your life?

Can you think of some generational sins that have been passed down through your family?

What sins are you holding onto? Will you repent and allow God's forgiveness to pour over you today?

_____

_____

_____

_____

_____

_____

_____

_____

_____

_____

_____

_____

_____

_____

_____

_____

Prayer to God

Heavenly Father, thank you for defeating death just for me. Take hold of my thoughts, my heart, and my spirit. Today, I choose to love myself as you do and love others as you have asked me to. I ask that you take over my life and give me eyes to see, ears to hear Your voice, and to always feel Your presence. I ask that You forgive my sins. Sins of jealousy, envy, pride, self-loathing. Lies I tell myself and lies I tell other people.

Jesus, I believe You died on the cross for me and all the people who surround me. I believe Your blood covers all my sins and makes me a new creation in You. I know I have a new, perfect and pure bloodline in You.

I ask that You fill me with Your Holy Spirit, Your wisdom, and Your knowledge. I pray You give me the ability to do Your will, not my own. I pray Your love shines through me. Use me as an instrument in Your Body.

I ask that You make me a light that shines Your beauty, joy, love, and Your grace among all of Your beloved creations.

In Jesus' Name,

Amen.

deepening your walk

Scripture Verse

"For we are God's masterpiece. He has created
us anew in Christ Jesus, so we can do the good
things he planned for us long ago."

Ephesians 2:10 (NLT)

Translations

Key Words

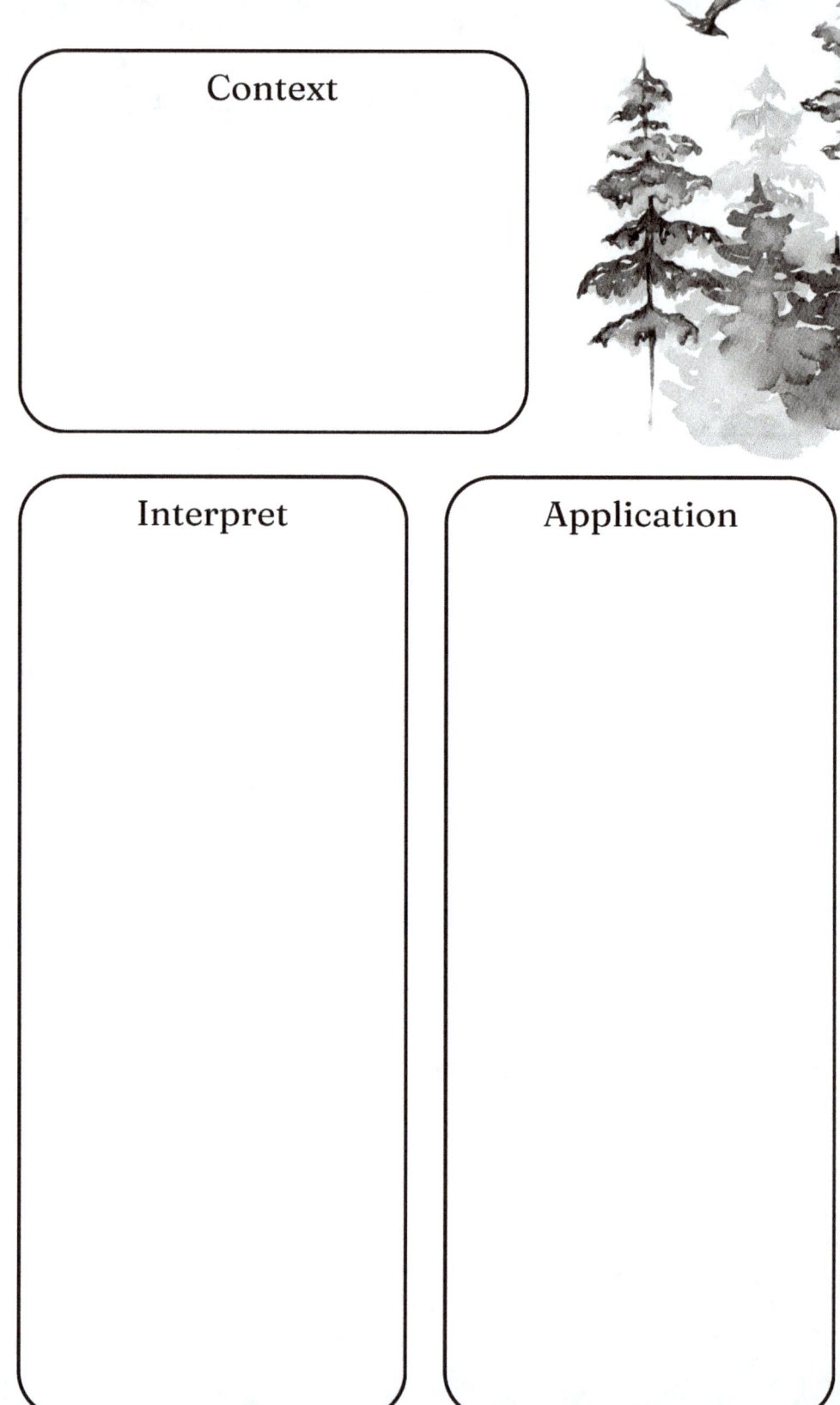

Context

Interpret

Application

redemption story

Tina Jacobson

> Jesus answered, "Everyone who drinks this water will be thirsty again, but whoever drinks the water I give them will never thirst. Indeed, the water I give them will become in them a spring of water welling up to eternal life."
>
> John 4:12-13 (NIV)

Woman at the Well

You may have heard the story or even remember it from your childhood. Jesus reached out to a woman at the well, knowing it was unacceptable between the cultures of Jews and Samaritans.

We know Jesus was traveling across a vast distance as he approached Samaria. He was tired from his long journey and sat down at Jacob's well. A Samaritan woman came to draw water, and Jesus asked her for a drink. The woman was surprised because Jews did not usually interact with Samaritans.

What did Jesus do? He told her about the "living water" only he could give, which would quench her thirst forever. This sounded foreign and strange to the woman. What did Jesus mean? How could this man she had just met provide this type of water—and without a bucket? Jesus shared even more with her.

Jesus revealed to her that he knew about her past: she had been married five times, and the man she was currently with was not her husband. This surprised the woman. Could this man be a prophet? She mentioned the coming of the Messiah, and Jesus revealed that he was the Messiah. How could this be?

The woman left her water jar, ran back to town, and told the people about Jesus, saying, "Come, see a man who told me everything I ever did. Could this be the Messiah?" Many Samaritans from the town believed in Jesus because of her testimony. They invited Jesus to stay with them, and after hearing him, many more believed, proclaiming Jesus as the Savior of the world.

What a miracle! It was one of the many that Jesus would do during his life on Earth. Yet, what does this story tell us? It meant acceptance, identity—and just as we see in many of Jesus' messages, it is about LOVE.

Have you ever felt like, "This is my journey with God?" After almost 24 years of being away from the church environment—unless it was for a wedding, funeral, or during extreme life events—I wasn't sure if God existed. I nearly lost belief in him.

But one morning, feeling overcome with loss and confusion, I chose to walk into a service of a church that I wasn't even familiar with. This particular day was very overwhelming and emotional. It took everything in me to not start crying as I sat and listened to the sermon. I felt God had led me to this particular church for a reason. I felt God was telling me I was going to be okay with the choice I had made of leaving my marriage of 22 years—one of the biggest and toughest decisions I have ever made in my life.

Have you heard a sermon that you knew was just for you in that given moment? Sitting there, I was the woman at the well.

I would like to share with you why this sermon meant so much to me and how it touched deep inside me.

It began while I was taking a class to become a certified coach. Much of the course was dedicated to personal reflection. One of the experiences was to self-reflect on our gifts, strengths, and uniqueness, as well as our weaknesses and struggles. I found this to be a massive challenge in itself. I had to work on these areas for a few weeks, because I wasn't sure where to begin. Should I look at my life, career, or marriage?

I reached out to my mentor, and we discussed where to begin and how to open up to those hidden hurts and memories, tucked away for so long. She stated, "Start by reflecting on your life and even consider those individuals you want to remain on the path with you." I sat with this for a few more days. And then one evening—I realized I didn't even recognize who I was anymore. I felt lost inside my own life.

The more I sat with my thoughts, the more I discovered I wasn't content at all with who I was or who I had become over the years. What had happened to me? I was depressed, introverted, closed-off, timid, excessively overweight, and completely unhappy with myself. I was living a lie with myself and even with others.

I pondered on these thoughts for months and kept

digging down as to why I was not content or even at peace with different areas in my life. We all know we can't change our past, but we sure can shift our future and the way we feel about ourselves, no matter what that may look like. It was at that moment that I realized it was me who needed to make the changes I wanted for myself.

There were numerous realizations. I have consistently been the person who said "yes" to everyone and everything. I was a people pleaser. Does this sound familiar to you? I realized how much time I wasted over the years doing things for others. Things that didn't align with my gifts and purpose that God wanted me to be accessing—all because I was afraid of losing a relationship, a job, or even myself.

Constantly taking care of other people and allowing others to dictate your actions may come at the expense of your own health, wellness, and stress level; relationships may become codependent and possibly lead to an unhealthy control situation.

Sit in this moment and reflect, lean in, and breathe. I want you to be true to yourself and your feelings. Ask the Lord in this moment: Where do YOU want me, God, and how can I serve You best? It is okay to have conflicting feelings, and more than likely, you will. Believe me—I know I did. It is a struggle when you finally admit what has taken hold of your life, just like the woman at the well. Jesus sees through it all.

I knew making any harsh and rash decisions was not an option for me. The consequences were too extreme, as you can imagine. I chose to listen to the Lord and walk with Him by my side. I knew God wanted me to be successful, empowering, and strong. Dedicated and devoted to Him. I could feel the newness of His Spirit within me because of His love, acceptance, and guidance through the Word.

There were changes I needed to make in my life to

receive the "peace that passes all understanding" through the Lord. If I could share one of my own life lessons with you, it would be this: stop listening to what others say to you and about you. Their words and judgment should not be your guide. Whether related to your job, your health, your relationship with friends, or significant others—God is your guide, not others' opinions and thoughts.

What do you need to get back to that reborn woman in the Lord?

What would your identity in Him look like?

I found these questions important to my own journey. Maybe they will be a support and encouragement to you.

"A fearless woman reclaims her power through the Lord, by choosing courage over comfort, embracing her path without regret, and trusting that every decision she makes with His guidance is a step toward her limitless potential."

tina jacobson

As you ease into your new understanding of who you are in Him, remember that the gentleness of self-care is important. Remember to embrace the simplicities in taking time for yourself; taking a long, luxurious bubble bath, getting your nails done, or maybe going on a long overdue date night to get that spark back into your relationship.

I found the habit of journaling daily supported me as I walked through the valleys and peaks of my life. I began working with a coach who aligned with me and my needs, so I was strengthened by the wisdom of the Lord with someone who is a "wise counsel." These may be helpful options for your journey as well.

Here is a quote I want you to really take a moment to sit and reflect on:

> A fearless woman reclaims her power through the Lord, by choosing courage over comfort, embracing her path without regret, and trusting that every decision she makes with His guidance is a step toward her limitless potential.
>
> *Tina Jacobson*

Take that leap of faith with God by your side and experience something that could be truly amazing. His Word tells us how precious we are to Him, how loved, and where we are needed to be for His glory in the Kingdom on Earth.

> Trust in the Lord completely, and do not rely on your own opinions. With all your heart, rely on Him to guide you, and He will lead you in whatever decision you make. Become intimate with him in whatever you do, and he will lead you wherever you go.
>
> Proverbs 3:5-6 (TPT)

The Lord "nudges" us to prepare a way forward in our lives. God wants you to be who He has created you to be. Take the leap of faith with Him guiding you. There may be struggles along the way, but you will be guided through them as the Lord navigates your steps forward.

The people you choose to bring along on this journey will see this transformation in you. If they are not supportive, it is time to evaluate their impact and influence in your life. Know it is okay to keep some relationships, but also set boundaries and honor the people in your life. God wants you to have connections with individuals who know Him and can support your walk of faith and even grow together.

> Discover creative ways to encourage others and to motivate them toward acts of compassion, doing beautiful works as expressions of love. This is not the time to pull away and neglect meeting together, as some have formed the habit of doing. In fact, we should come together even more frequently, eager to encourage and urge each other onward as we anticipate that day dawning.
>
> Hebrews 10:22-25 (TPT)

Over the past few years, I moved from Minnesota to Washington to Texas then back to Minnesota. I did it to be close to family and support my aging parents. Little did I know there was going to be so much more in store during this season of my life that would change me forever. I could see the Hand of God guiding me through a series of events, even though devastating and rewarding, all at the same time.

One of the first experiences was when He led me to what I thought was a temporary job—but it turned out to be a step closer back to God. The owners of the company were Christians, and created an environment where faith was important. We prayed every Monday morning for our co-workers who traveled, our farmers, and family members who needed it. It was a refreshing atmosphere to come into. Even with business challenges, we always worked through them together. Through my own healing, I was able to help employees and guide them through some of the challenges that arose. God put me here for a reason and I knew it. As time has gone on, I realize He has guided me in ways I couldn't have imagined.

When we accept that we have choices in life, we do not have to feel stuck in any given situation. The Lord will bring us through the tough times of the past and present to lead us right into this particular moment. Yes, we need to take accountability for our past and learn from the mistakes we may have made. Yet, regret is not of the Lord.

He asks us to give it all to Him, just like the woman at the well. That is what I started doing.

Can you sit back and think about a time when you did something or maybe said something out of spite or anger—and then regretted it later?

Our words have strength and even direction, no matter where they are aimed. In Proverbs, the Bible states, "there is power in the tongue." Going to the Lord first and asking for the words and actions He wants you to share—or sometimes not share—is honoring Him. Why wouldn't you want to do the same thing in a career choice?

Perhaps you have a job where you show up to honor the company and the position, yet you have a boss who is disrespectful to you and abuses their power to make you feel less than. Remember in Proverbs 27:17 (NIV), "Iron sharpens iron," and in all of our relationships, we must seek out those that follow biblical principles to align ourselves with as a mentor or possibly as a boss.

I learned that walking in truth and honor of my position and with others is an important step to being healthy in jobs and careers. Seeking wise counsel in these situations is where we can continue to walk a path God has us on for His glory. The Bible tells us that "the righteous choose their friends carefully..." in Proverbs 12:26 (NIV). He means all of them, whether it is a friendship or an acquaintance in our life or work.

"God is going to equip you to shine in your unique purpose, even through difficult times."

tina jacobson

To accomplish this, I found I needed to examine all of the relationships I was currently in.

The outcome was eye-opening. Now, it is your turn.

Make a list of key people in your life. Ask yourself these questions:

- How do they have an influence in my life?
- Do they have an impact, too?
- How do they walk alongside me during the hard times and not just the good times?
- What boundaries do I have in place with each of them?
- What do you give or add into their life? What do they give or add into your life?

> She wraps herself in strength; might, and power in all her works. She tastes and experiences a better substance, and her shining light will not be extinguished, no matter how dark the night. She stretches out her hands to the needy and she lays hold of the wheels of government.
>
> Proverbs 31:17-18 (TPT)

This will be a reflection of God's guidance and partnership in your journey, enabling you to walk with dignity and face challenges with confidence. God is going to equip you to shine in your unique purpose, even through difficult times. You are a woman of incredible strength and dignity, and God has clothed you in these gifts to face whatever challenges come your way. As you walk through this journey, know that He is with you, guiding your steps and filling your heart with wisdom.

You have the ability to stand tall, speak with grace and courage, and inspire those around you. Even in tough times, your laughter and hope reflect a faith that cannot be shaken. Trust in the Lord's presence by your side, and continue to let His light shine through you in everything you do.

You are a beacon of resilience and love. Keep moving forward with confidence—you are walking in His purpose and plan.

What is holding you back from being the best YOU for the Lord?

As you lean into a new focus on being more purposeful and resilient in your life for the Lord, ask yourself these questions:

- What are my next steps with and for God?

- Where do I want to walk closer with Him and through what actions?

- What things am I holding on to from your previous life that are becoming obstacles?

- Do I feel "equally yoked" (2 Corinthians 6:14, NIV) with the people and their actions in my life?

- Do I have an accountability partner and a "wise counsel" in my life aligned with God?

- How am I continuing to grow in the Lord and in my life?

In his book, *Fifty Shades of They*, Pastor Ed Young talks about examining those individuals in your life in three categories to support your desire to have Godly connections and community.

"For You"—people who appear to be your greatest supporters until a conflict or obstacle happens and they react negatively to you.

"Use You"—people who get too close only when it is something for them to gain so they can continually excel in their own life and work.

"With You"—people who truly walk with you through the tough times and support you in every interaction. They will also let you know when you are off your walk with the Lord and not judge you, but give you guidance while you are finding your way back and through the difficulties.

> "You have the ability to stand tall, speak with grace and courage, and inspire those around you."
> *tina jacobson*

Do you feel that you have lost your voice with others? Have you shifted away from childhood friends who you were close to you, but now you no longer talk to? Have you ever found yourself lying to others to cover up what is truly happening in your life? Have you pulled away from friends and family, you stopped doing things that you once enjoyed in life? Sometimes, you may not even remember that happy, funny outgoing person you once were. Then, you look back at all the friends you once had, and wonder where they all went. It is time to take back control of the decisions you are making in your life and surround yourself with the Godly aligned "they."

> God, the searcher of the heart, fully knows our longings, yet he also understands the desire of the Spirit, because the Holy Spirit passionately pleads before God for us, his holy ones, in perfect harmony with God's plan and our destiny… Who then would dare to accuse those whom God has chosen in love to be his? God himself is the judge who has issued his final verdict over them— "not guilty." … Who then is left to condemn us?
>
> Romans 8:27, 33, 34 (TPT)

You are never done learning who you are and what your purpose is for God on this earth. I have found new things about myself that I never knew that existed, and God has been the One who has guided me through my life—especially over the last two years. He has given me the strength I didn't know I had to leave a 22-year marriage that was filled with narcissism, manipulation, and control—to step out on my own for the first time. I am learning all about myself again; how to appreciate the right relationships and reject the others, and find a peace I didn't know I could have.

You may be content and appreciate every part of your life just as it is. Yet, maybe there is something you feel you are missing. Perhaps it could be that you just need to find God again and walk alongside Him in the journey to healing; something from your past that is holding you back from who the Lord sees in you.

We all have some kind of trauma or struggle deep down that may need resolution. It could be something that has even caused a fear. We just need to find out what those emotions and memories are and release them. Once you have let go, you will find that you are going to be more joyful and feel vibrant again.

Although you have hills and valleys in your life, know that you will come out the other side of things, as you allow the Lord to create the new you. Walk firmly and humbly with Him. Be AT the well and Jesus will know you, see you, and love you.

> Therefore, if anyone is in Christ, the new creation has come: The old has gone, the new is here!
>
> 2 Corinthians 5:17 (NIV)

Reflection

What burdens from my past am I still carrying, and how are they affecting my ability to step into healing and freedom?

If I fully believed that God sees me, loves me, and calls me worthy, how would my life begin to change?

What is one step I can take today to release my past and embrace the healing and freedom God is offering me?

_____

_____

_____

_____

_____

_____

_____

_____

_____

_____

_____

_____

_____

_____

_____

_____

Prayer to God

Heavenly Father,

I come before You today, thirsty for Your presence, just as the woman at the well stood before Jesus—worn, weary, and longing for something more. You see me, Lord. You know my past, my wounds, my burdens. And yet, You do not turn away. Instead, You draw near, offering me Living Water that heals, restores, and sets me free.

I release the pain I have carried for too long—the shame, the regrets, the weight of what has been. I lay it at Your feet, knowing that in You, I am not defined by my past but by Your love and grace. Wash over me, Lord. Heal the wounds that run deep, the ones that words could never explain but You fully understand.

I choose freedom today. I choose to step out of the shadows of yesterday and into the light of Your truth. You call me beloved. You call me whole. You call me worthy. And today, I choose to believe You.

Fill me, Lord, with Your peace, with the courage to walk forward, and with the faith to trust that You are making all things new within me. Let my life be a testimony of Your redemption—a story of a woman who was broken but now is healed, who was bound but now is free.

Thank You, Jesus, for meeting me here. I receive Your love, and I step forward, renewed, restored, and ready to walk in the purpose You have for me.

In Jesus' name,

Amen.

deepening your walk

Scripture Verse

"Jesus answered, 'Everyone who drinks this water will be thirsty again, but whoever drinks the water I give them will never thirst. Indeed, the water I give them will become in them a spring of water welling up to eternal life.'"

John 4:12-13 (NIV)

Translations

Key Words

Context

Interpret

Application

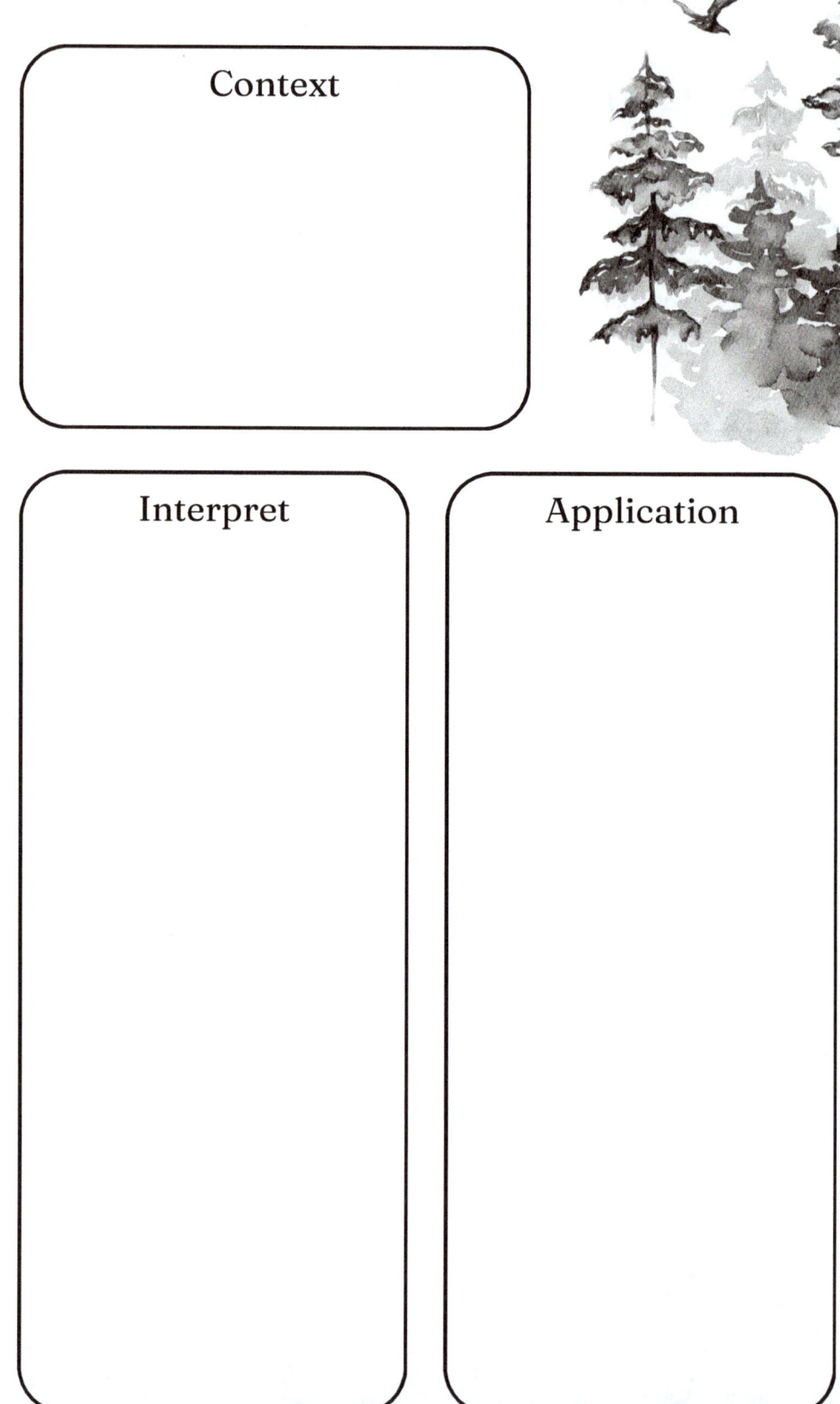

seasons of grace

Mantequilla Green

> The LORD is close to the brokenhearted and saves those who are crushed in spirit.
>
> Psalm 34:18 (NIV)

Grief. Loss. Anger. Fear. Helplessness. Uncertainty. Sadness.

Have you ever gone through seasons of your life and questioned, "Who am I? What has happened to my life? How did I get here?" During the span of just three short years, I felt this way to my very core. Numbness. Hurt. Confusion.

I was overwhelmed and unsupported. I was devastated. And I was ripped apart by the root of my soul.

Have you ever been there?

November 2007

As a teacher, I was feeling better than ever. My students and I were bonding and making great progress. We published our first newspaper—in color! Football games had started. The photography staff would attend the games to shoot pictures. Each Monday, my first period English class and I would have "Football Monday." We discussed the high school game and the Dallas Cowboys game, as they both had amazing seasons that year. It was so much fun!

One Monday as we were discussing the games, I received a phone call from who I thought was my dad. Only it wasn't my dad—it was my cousin calling from my dad's phone to inform me that my father had passed away. I thought maybe Dad had a stroke or heart attack, as he had suffered a massive stroke the previous year. But it turned out my father had taken his life. I was devastated; it felt as if my body went into shock immediately. I could not comprehend how we had gotten here, how my dad felt he needed to take his own life.

I hung up the phone and looked at my students, unsure what to do. So, I made the decision to continue teaching—even after I told them that my dad had passed. They looked at me with amazement in their eyes.

When class was over, all 25 students lined up to give me a hug and their condolences before they left. For them, it was heartfelt and compassionate. For me, I was touched, but sadly numb—and still processing what had just happened.

I stayed through the day to prepare for a substitute teacher to take my place for a week. I told my other classes about my father's passing and what my expectations were for the week I would be gone. Once all my classes were completed for the day, I headed home. It was the longest, loneliest drive I had ever driven.

Suddenly, I didn't want to be at home alone. Before my dad passed, I considered myself somewhat of a loner and loved solitude. This time, I wanted to be around people. I couldn't sleep or eat. I just wanted company.

My dear friend, Katie, came over and stayed with me all night. I never slept more than 20 minutes at a time. Sleeping had never been a problem for me, but suddenly, I wasn't comfortable in my own bedroom, even in the new, cozy bed I had recently bought.

Most people had the same questions. What happened? What was my dad going through before he took his life? Had he been depressed? While I knew a little of what my dad was experiencing (a massive stroke, a struggle to heal, going on disability, etc.), I never knew the extent of all he endured.

The night after my dad died, my stepmom called. I hadn't talked to her for many years. It wasn't because I didn't love her; it was because my dad didn't like us being close. So, she and I both avoided talking to each other. "I just wanted to tell you how sorry I am about your dad," she said. "If I had been there, I could have stopped him."

Puzzled, I said to her, "I'm grateful that you left my dad (she had left him three weeks prior). If you hadn't, we would be burying him here and going to Mississippi to bury you."

Immediately after the conversation, it felt like our closeness had been restored. I believe we both felt it. She and I were kindred spirits, in some kind of odd way. This tragedy had united us.

I tended to sleep during the day while I was out on bereavement leave. I started to pray that God would help us get through this tough time as a family. I was still asking God, "How did we get here?" Soon, Friday came. I felt the Holy Spirit leading me to travel home.

I was stunned by what happened that day. When I arrived two and a half hours later, I learned that my older brother, youngest sister, and my stepmom were all waiting at the house for me to arrive; we had all arrived on the same day! My stepmom convinced her mom and sister to take her to the home she shared with my father because she knew that's where we would go. Within an hour, my brother and sister showed up. Half an hour later, I arrived. In conversations with my brother, I mentioned that we needed to be together—just the children and our stepmom, to process what happened. My brother felt it wouldn't happen until after the service, but it was happening before we even planned the service. God is so amazing! He was listening to our conversations and answering prayers!

While I was there, I had to make some decisions related to my dad's death about things that I didn't really want to know. For example, he left a note, and our cousin who dealt with the police had a copy of it. I decided I didn't want to read it. I also didn't want to go into the room where he was found. Unfortunately, I didn't win that one. So, we all entered the room, which had been cleaned by HazMat. And God was so gracious in that moment. I simply couldn't imagine my dad in that room. But I did notice a collection of hats my dad liked to wear. One hat in particular caught my eye. Of all my dad's hats, it was my favorite.

My dad's service was the following Monday. When I saw the hearse, that's when reality hit me. It hadn't seemed real, but now it was. I didn't want to go through with it. But, the Holy Spirit reassured me that God was with me and I could continue. I had been praying that we would have a good service for my dad. I didn't want him to have a long, dragging, sad service.

When I approached the church, I saw the pastor. It turns out he and I grew up together and spent summers at the East Texas Baptist Congress. We were a part of the youth department and took courses together during the week. He sang in the choir. I participated in the Bible drill competition, where I received several trophies. We were both stunned to see each other, as it had been close to 20 years since we last saw each other. However, he was a great comfort to my family and me as we grieved so much for my dad. He made sure that his service did not go over for an extended time and he allowed the immediate family private time to say goodbye, just us with my dad. God's grace was over us.

The following day, it was time to return to Dallas. I went by my dad's house one more time to say good-bye to my stepmom. In my heart, it felt like I wasn't going to see her again. She gave me a plant that was sent to me by some friends. Then, I saw my favorite hat. Lovingly, my aunt gave it to me. My stepmom gave me pictures of my dad that were just taken a month before his death. I saw his fresh grave on the way home, and it pierced my soul. For the first time, I cried over losing my father and I felt the aching type of hurt that comes from deep down inside.

The next day was Wednesday, and I went back to work. I had asked the principal if I could have the week off, as the next week would be Thanksgiving break. My thought was after three weeks, I should be more emotionally prepared to return to work. However, my principal never answered my email and I had no other way to contact her. So, I returned to work.

I was numb that day. I didn't want to be there. No one understood my agony, especially since I had made it known that he was an absent father. This was one of those times when I needed the powers-that-be to look beyond the needs of students and see my needs, but it didn't happen. So I taught.

In the midst of all my pain, I kept teaching and encouraging my students. Still, I couldn't act like nothing had happened. I needed to be there for them as much as I could. Education can sometimes be unforgiving to the struggles of teachers. But, because teachers care so much about their students, they, like parents, brush aside their needs to make sure their students' needs are met.

When I returned home that evening, I opened the door and lay prostrate on the floor. "Lord, I'm hurting," I said. "I'm in uncharted territory as I have never lost a parent. I don't know what to pray for. All I know is that I'm hurting." I prayed that prayer every morning and every day before and after work. I would awake each morning at 4:30 a.m., get dressed, pray, and leave for work. I would listen to Beth Moore's "Fruit of the Spirit" series on the way to work and arrive at 6:30 every morning. School didn't start until 8:45. When I arrived, I would do whatever work I was behind on.

I still stayed after school, except for when I needed to see my grief counselor. My friend, Katie, suggested that I should go to counseling due to the nature of my dad's death. So, I did.

Counseling was uncomfortable at first, as I had never gone before. But, I knew I needed to unpack how my dad arrived at his decision, as well as processing our relationship. I needed to know if I would ever smile again. Initially, I was going to counseling weekly, but I started to improve. So, the counselor switched me to bi-monthly appointments. God was beginning to heal me.

Blessed are those who mourn, for they will be comforted.
Matthew 5:4 (NIV)

In this profession I have chosen, sometimes we go through the loss of a youth or work with them through their own struggles. It could be their parents are on drugs or not emotionally present. It could be that one parent was murdered and they are navigating life without them.

But I have found that losing someone from suicide is a different type of pain. The grief is deep. There are questions that can't be answered. There's no trial and no conclusion of what actually occurred. Going through these types of highly emotional situations can take any professional to their knees—but they can bring healing even through painful and debilitating circumstances.

December 2007

I think I had only seen my counselor for one bi-monthly appointment when I learned that my best friend, Katie—my dear friend who had been with me through my father's death—had passed away. I was in utter shock. Katie had just visited me the weekend before. I talked to her three days prior to her death on Thursday. When I called on Friday, she wouldn't answer her phone—and by Sunday, I realized she never would again. All of a sudden, I was back at the devastating and overwhelming feelings I had when my dad died. But now—I was grieving two people.

Katie's death felt like my soul was pulled out by its root. I couldn't breathe. I didn't know how I was going to live without my best friend. Lord, how could this be happening? The pain was deep and cutting, ripped open from the fresh wounds that were just showing the start of healing. Katie's passing was sudden. She was transitioning from a career as a nurse into nurse consulting. She was full of anticipation, excited for what God would do in the next season of her life.

After the deaths of my dad and Katie, my body began to show signs of stress as it never had before. My blood pressure spiked. I was rushed to the emergency room because I couldn't keep anything down. Doctors found that my white blood cell count was elevated.

Again, God was so gracious to me during this time. My neighbors, church members, new friends, and many others gathered around to help me get through this dark time. They brought meals, gave me books to read, and checked on me. I appreciated all of the gestures, but I didn't know how to tell them to help me. I didn't even know what kind of help I needed.

"Lord, thank you for getting me through today. But I'm still hurting."

mantequilla green

I continued counseling. It was the one time I could talk about what I was going through. I couldn't pray, because I honestly didn't know what to pray. All I would say is "Lord, I'm hurting."

I went to work each day, and when I would arrive home after work, I would immediately lie prostrate on the floor and pray, "Lord, thank you for getting me through today. But I'm still hurting."

> Weeping may endure for a night, but a shout of joy comes in the morning.
>
> Psalm 30:5b (AMP)

School Year 2006-2007

Through it all, I was teaching at a well-known charter school. Leading students through teaching had long been a passion and calling of mine. My journey as a teacher would sometimes hit a crossroads as I made decisions between following a leader versus, at times, my commitment to God and the call He placed on my life. This often led to the choice of whether to compromise and please my leader or stand firm and please God. Standing firm to please God could potentially lead to losing a job or losing a responsibility I enjoyed. However, I have seen God redeem me in these situations. You can imagine the dilemmas that were created with this directive in my life.

There were times when the program I oversaw suffered because a leader made a choice to remove me from a position where I was prospering in favor of a plan that he or she thought was more prosperous—but it was not. The only action I could take was to pray for them and leave the situation in God's hand. I would also ask God to let me prosper where He planted me until He chose to move me forward.

God opened the door for our school to partner with a local TV station to start a student broadcast. Because I was certified in journalism, my principal, who was a believer in Christ, wanted me to oversee the program under his guidance. Our first encounter with this program was amazing! Our students got the opportunity to work with professional journalists from the *Dallas Morning News* and *The Fort Worth Star Telegram* and other well-known journalists. The students' first newscast was broadcast across the district. We had pioneered something genuinely special—along with the remarkable students who may not have otherwise had the opportunity to experience journalism.

Shortly after our success, our supportive principal left, and an interim principal took over. This person was not a visionary as we had been used to under our previous principal. So, I not only lost a principal who had the same values and beliefs as me, but the new principal seemed to care more about "appearances." Many of us lived under the constant threat of termination—so we gave up trying to build relationships. The fledgling and successful journalism program we started was quickly suspended.

This was a stressful time for me, so much so that I became ill with chronic migraine headaches. I went to the doctor and was prescribed medication—but it didn't work. When I prayed, God comforted me by assuring me that He would protect me through the school year—but it was not without turbulence.

Adding to my stressful load, I was moved out of my comfort zone and asked to be a substitute administrator when the principal was out. I had never received training as an administrator. On days in which I was the administrator, I would ask for a substitute to take my classes so I could walk the building. I would send out prayer requests to my strongest prayer warriors. And God would prevail every time. I felt His calming and reassuring presence with me as I walked the halls. His grace was in the school.

Near the end of the year, the interim principal nominated me for campus Teacher of the Year. Those nominated were required to film a lesson and submit essays to the judges, who were Dallas Baptist University professors. Each campus Teacher of the Year nominee was considered a finalist. This would mean that whoever of us was chosen would be the teacher of the year for the entire statewide conglomerate, which was no small achievement!

The interim principal was very cold toward me at the Teacher of the Year luncheon. Upon my win, she didn't congratulate me. She did, however, send an email to the staff after school was finished for the day—and when the whole staff would be outside for dismissal. One staff member saw the email and came out screaming at the top of his lungs, celebrating the victory. To him, winning Teacher of the Year recognized not just me, but the entire school—especially after such a turbulent year. I was more than happy to share the victory!

About a week after winning the Teacher of the Year, the interim principal offered me a job in another state. This was her way of removing me from campus. I didn't understand. How do you justify terminating the Teacher of the Year? I turned down her offer, because through seeking God's wisdom and discernment, I was shown that she did not mean well. Later, God allowed me to learn that she never wanted me to receive the prestigious Teacher of the Year award. But, God had other plans. His grace prevailed.

> When the enemy comes in like a flood, the Spirit of the Lord shall lift up a standard against him.
>
> Isaiah 59:19 (NIV)

I reflected and meditated on this scripture a lot during my tenure at this school. It was the only way I could endure the tough times. Most of the time, I would close my classroom door during lunch to pray and read the Word. It kept me sane.

By the end of the year, I knew I would not return; the constant chaos surrounding the school was simply too much. Most of our staff, including our principal, had left to accept greater opportunities. I couldn't see how the current leadership at the charter school would benefit our students or staff—so I left.

School Year 2007-2008

Before long, God had planted me at a new school. This time, the school was 15 minutes away from my home. The new job consisted of teaching mostly journalism courses and two English classes. The interview was beyond expectations; it was wonderful! However, I wasn't certified in English, so the interviewer didn't believe she could hire me. After researching and finding that college journalism courses count as English courses, they called and made an offer. When I signed the contract, I also signed an agreement that I would be certified by the end of the school year.

On the first day of school, I walked into a large classroom. It was a teacher's dream! For the first time, I had my own office, a darkroom, and a traditional newsroom that had cutting boards and lighting tables. It even had a working full-size refrigerator! Lisa was one of my first students to walk into the classroom. She was a beautiful young lady, walking with the help of crutches and escorted by her boyfriend, Duke. She told me she had torn ligaments at cheer camp. I certainly knew her struggle, as I spent a summer on crutches from an ankle fusion surgery when I was 12.

My students were amazing! My classes were easier to teach than I could imagine. In fact, they could nearly run themselves. They were such fast learners and there was so much diversity. This school had equal percentages of every ethnicity. It was the first time I worked in an extremely diverse school, in a somewhat affluent neighborhood.

I often thought, "This must be what Heaven looks like!" They learned I liked football and would invite me to the games, and I would happily attend. The journalism students stayed after school every Tuesday and Wednesday. So, we began to get to know each other, and the students and I bonded quickly and deeply.

At some point during the grieving process, I thought about my students and the fact that they would take the state exam soon. So, I added to my prayer, "Lord, I'm hurting. But, please don't allow my students to suffer because I'm suffering."

I walked my students through the steps of how to take the state exam for Texas about two weeks before testing. On the day of the test, each teacher was assigned their own duties to help administer the test. When the students were done testing, we had classes in the afternoon (we only shut down for half of the day for testing).

Lisa walked into class highly disturbed. She approached my desk quietly.

"Ms. Green, you're going to jail!" She said in a whispered tone.

"Why do you think that?" I asked.

"Do you remember the lesson you taught on how to take the test a few weeks ago?" she asked. "Ms. Green, all the questions you went over with us were on the test. I almost lost it during the test. I told my friend sitting next to me that I think my teacher committed a crime!"

I laughed hysterically! This was a belly laugh, tears flowing, a kind of laugh that you can't stop no matter how hard you try. It was a laugh I desperately needed after experiencing such heavy grief.

"Sweetheart, I'm not going to jail," I managed to say while still laughing. "We are not allowed to view the test. The only reason we actively monitor is to ensure that you are working on the right section of the test. If we are caught having knowledge of the test, that is a crime. It appears that the makers of the test used questions that have been used before, probably in a different format."

"Whew!" she sighed. "I'm glad to hear that! I was really scared for a minute. I really didn't know what to do. But, you should be proud of yourself because I think we all did well."

"God did not allow my students to suffer even though I was suffering. He heard me."

mantequilla green

When the results came, Lisa was right in her prediction. Out of 53 English students, 27 of them scored commended, which was the highest grade a student could achieve on the test. God did not allow my students to suffer even though I was suffering. He heard me.

At the end of the year, after all God had done, I learned that I would no longer serve at this school. Remember how I was supposed to be certified by the end of the school year? Well, I wasn't certified by the beginning of March, which was the district's deadline. I was certified the following month. However, the principal took that time to hire a new teacher without my knowledge—even though it had been agreed upon that once I was certified, I would reapply for the position and be rehired. But, God was faithful.

Once I learned I no longer had that job, a school in Dallas contacted me for an interview. They were searching specifically for me to the point they called my mother. When I went to the interview, I was told, "Their loss is our gain." That was refreshing to hear. By this time in my career, I wondered if I was really called to teach.

The next four years would be some of the most amazing years of my life. I taught Pre-Advanced Placement (AP) and AP courses and loved it! My passion for teaching was re-ignited. While these students lived in West Dallas, which was the worst part of Dallas at the time, they were some of the brightest students I'd had the pleasure to teach. We were inspired by each other. They wanted to see my degrees, so they asked me to hang them on the wall by my desk where they would be visible to the students each day.

While teaching there, I started working on my master's degree. My professors would have us writing 5-10 page papers on various topics. One topic was about a tragic event that occurred and how we got through it. Of course, I wrote about my dad's passing. I found writing about that time in my life was cathartic.

I went to grief counseling until October, just one month shy of the anniversary of my father's death. When we finished the session that day, the counselor looked at me and said, "There's nothing wrong with you. You don't have to come back anymore." While I was thrilled to hear that I was done with counseling, I knew I wasn't done healing. What I was grateful for was the simple prayer of "Lord, I'm hurting," and while listening to Beth Moore— God answered. I could smile again. I could have a lucid thought again, and the numbness and fogginess had lifted.

I realized holding onto scriptures like Psalms 34:18 (NIV) helped save me: "God is close to the brokenhearted and saves those who are crushed in spirit." Reading books like Tony Dungy's Quiet Strength helped me process my grief, specifically as a survivor of a loved one who took his life. Going to counseling helped me unpack my relationship with my dad. My dad confided in me a lot, but we also argued a lot. Yet, because of my walk with the Lord, my father sought me out for advice. I didn't understand why. But, now I understand that perhaps my dad felt comfortable and unjudged in telling me his deepest thoughts while he sought what God wanted for him. It gave me comfort that for some reason, my dad trusted me in ways that he would never express.

Within the next two years, my uncle and grandmother

both passed away. My grandmother, Mama Mae, had an emergency surgery that led to severe complications. When she started to transition a week after surgery, what I saw was God restoring her vitals, while surrounding her with family and his love. There were several days in which my youngest brother would play Christian music for her, my youngest uncle would read scripture aloud to her, and my mom and I would sing some of her favorite hymns. In all the deaths that occurred, Mama Mae's was the sweetest. My perspective was not, "Lord, why are you taking her?" but was more, "She's served her purpose, it's time to go see Jesus and gain her reward." While I miss her, I am grateful for the way she helped raise us, four of her youngest grandchildren, as unto the Lord. 2 Corinthians 5:8 (NIV) comforted me: "We are of good courage and confident hope, and prefer rather to be absent from the body and be home with the Lord."

Through each of these seasons, I've learned God is faithful and He is a God of restoration. He hears our deepest cries and He will be there to help us through our toughest times. We will all walk through grief; loss of loved ones, jobs, churches, relationships. But—no matter how tough letting go is, God is there and He "will never leave us nor forsake us." Hebrews 13:5 (NIV). Therefore, I am focused. I am strengthened. And I am restored.

"Through each of these seasons, I've learned God is faithful and He is a God of restoration."

mantequilla green

And I've learned that once we are on the other side of healing, God is faithful in exchanging "beauty for ashes and strength for despair" Isaiah 61:3 (NIV). By God's grace, I have been presented with opportunities to share my grief and healing experiences with others, in order to encourage them. Sometimes, the assignment is to recognize suicidal ideation in a student and ensure that they get help. Other times, it's supporting a school or church family by being who they need during the time.

In the past year, I have supported families and teachers in their times of grief by being the administrator that I needed to have when I was at my lowest. These divine assignments, specifically chosen by God for me, serve to keep me humbled and provide more healing—for which I will always be grateful.

Reflection

How has my life changed since my loss?

What unexpected emotions have surfaced during my grief?

How am I treating myself during the grieving process?

How have my relationships with others changed since my loss?

How am I different now compared to before the loss?

What new lessons have I learned about God during this time of grief?

Woodie, R. J. (2025, March 17). 30 Grief Reflection Questions. Apttones.com. March 17, 2025, https://apttones.com/grief-reflection-questions

_____

_____

_____

_____

_____

_____

_____

_____

_____

_____

_____

_____

_____

Prayer to God

Father, thank you for who You are. Thank You for being the One who consoles me.

Thank You for being the One who gives me peace, even in the middle of my darkest storm.

Thank You for never letting darkness consume me. Thank You for allowing me to see You in every grievous situation that occurs. Thank You for exchanging my ashes for Your beauty and giving me Your joy for my pain. It is because of You that I receive new grace, mercy, and healing every day.

For those who are experiencing the worst grief of their lives (a child, a spouse, a parent, a grandparent, etc.), please be close to their broken hearts, and save those who are crushed in spirit. Help them draw close to You and, as You promise, You will draw close to them. Help them see You in the middle of their grief and recognize that You have not left them nor have You forsaken them. Please send people to help give them strength and help them gain clarity. Please let them know they are not alone.

In Jesus' Name,

Amen.

deepening your walk

Scripture Verse

"So they will fear the name of the Lord from the west
And His glory from the rising of the sun.
For He will come in like a narrow, rushing stream
Which the breath of the Lord drives [overwhelming the enemy]."
Isaiah 59:19 (AMP)

Translations

Key Words

Context

Interpret

Application

finding your god-given purpose through the storms of life

Crystal Duncan-Hogue

> For we are his workmanship, created in Christ Jesus for good works, which God prepared beforehand, that we should walk in them.
>
> Ephesians 2:10 (ESV)

Everyone has experienced a storm in their life at some point. You may be at the beginning of one, in the middle, or perhaps nearing the end of it. If you haven't encountered any of these yet, I hate to be the bearer of bad news, but one might be lurking just around the corner. When a storm arrives suddenly, what do you do? How do you handle it? These are questions many of us wrestle with when the winds begin to howl and the sky darkens.

But amidst the chaos, I believe there is something greater at work, something that can reveal your true divine purpose. Life's storms are not merely obstacles; they are opportunities to discover what you were truly created for. It's easy to lose sight of this when the clouds obscure our vision, but I believe that our God-given purpose is there. What is the thing that stirs your soul? What drives you when everything else feels uncertain?

We are all here for a reason—to thrive in our God-given purpose. Every storm we face has the power to refine us, to help us see more clearly the path we are meant to walk. We must confront the question: Are we truly living in our God-given purpose? Or are we letting the storms blur our vision?

According to the Merriam-Webster dictionary, a storm is described as a disturbance of the atmosphere, typically accompanied by wind, rain, snow, hail, sleet, or thunder and lightning. A storm is a powerful, sometimes destructive force of nature, with winds reaching speeds between 64 and 72 miles per hour. It's a force that creates chaos and disrupts the natural flow of life, leaving behind damage, confusion, and uncertainty. We're familiar with these natural disaster-type storms—those physical storms that bring us to our knees, which leave us huddled in our homes, seeking shelter from the violence of the elements.

Have you ever wondered about the storms that come into our lives without warning? The kind of storm that can't be tracked on a radar, but instead arrives suddenly, seemingly out of nowhere. These storms don't always have wind or rain, but they carry a weight of their own.

What about those big obstacles that appear in your path, blocking your vision and making it impossible to see clearly? You know, the moments when life takes a sudden turn, and you're faced with a challenge that seems too great to overcome. The kind of storms that blind you to the future, leaving you feeling stuck and hopeless. You try to move forward, but the path is blocked by a rock, something heavy, something solid, something you can't budge no matter how hard you try. And in that moment, you stop and ask yourself, "Why keep going? Why keep pushing forward when this storm is so fierce and this obstacle is too large?"

You look around and see others in your circle—your friends, your family, who seem to be navigating their own storms with ease. They are moving forward, their faith unwavering—so it appears—walking on water while a storm rages around you. Perhaps this storm, the one you're facing right now, is not an accident. Could it be that this particular storm, the one that's so difficult to bear, was allowed by the Creator Himself? God, the supreme being who is to be worshiped, the One who spoke the world into existence and said, "Let there be light" (Genesis 1:3, ESV). The same God who has mastery over every storm, every cloud, every drop of rain, and every bolt of lightning. The same God who knows the exact nature of the storm you're in right now has allowed it for a specific reason. Could it be that this storm is part of a divine purpose, something greater than your immediate understanding?

Even so, the raging storm just doesn't seem to go away. In fact, it's worse than before. The storm has tossed you deeper into the ocean, and now thick darkness surrounds you on all sides. You're sinking, consumed by the weight of despair, the waves of life pulling you further under. As you descend into the depths, the cold, dark water pressing against you, you hear it—a voice, soft and steady, whispering through the chaos, "Come to me" (Matthew

11:28, ESV), "and I will set you free" (John 8:32, ESV).

Wait... What? Who said that?

It's then that you realize, this voice, this call, is none other than the One who has always been with you in the storm. The One who was sleeping on the boat with his head comfortably on a soft pillow when the winds howled and the waves crashed around you. The One who walked on the water with you through the tempest and who asked, "O ye of little faith, why did you doubt?"

> "It's then that you realize, this voice, this call, is none other than the One who has always been with you in the storm."
>
> *crystal duncan hogue*

And you were the one who stepped out of the boat, trusting His call, walking toward Him on the water despite the raging storm. You kept your eyes on Him and for a moment—you were walking in the miraculous. But then, you saw the waves, the boisterous winds (Matthew 14:30, ESV), so you took your eyes off Him. In that moment of distraction, the storm pulled you under. You cry out. And just like before, He hears you. With one swift motion, His strong right hand, filled with power, reaches down into the depths and pulls you from the water. His presence reassured you that the storm will not last forever.

Remember this: you are more than a conqueror through Jesus Christ (Romans 8:37, ESV). You have been given a light in this dark, stormy world. Yes, even in the midst of a dark storm, your light cannot be hidden under a bushel (Matthew 5:15, ESV). It is a gift—His light— Jesus Christ, shining within you. That light will lead you out of the dark storm. It will catch you when you fall, hold your hand, and walk with you in the cool of the day, giving you the strength to go through every trial.

Your Testimony

When you share your journey, your struggles, your pain—and the steps you took to overcome it, you just don't know how powerful your words can be to someone who needs to hear them. When you open your heart and share your story, it has the potential to change someone else's life. You can help them rise above their circumstances and help them discover their own purpose while at the same time, healing yourself. It's as if the very act of reflecting on your journey unearths something new within you, something you hadn't seen before.

Digging deeper within yourself can reveal hidden truths, guiding you to the realization that you are more than just a survivor of life's storms—you are a daughter of a King. And not just any king, but the King of Kings and the Lord of Lords. Understanding who you are, and whose you are, is foundational in finding your God-given purpose. You belong to God. You are a royal priesthood, an ambassador for Christ. You are chosen and loved beyond measure.

Do you realize that, as a daughter of the King, you have the right to cry out in your storm, "Abba Father" and say, "Daddy, here I am. Hold me and do not let me go. Please don't take Your Spirit from me; lead me in the path of righteousness for Your name's sake." In the darkest valleys, when the shadows seem to close in on every side, you can stand firm in the truth that you can fear no evil because He is with you. His rod, His staff comforts you. He has prepared a table before you, right in the midst of your enemies. You can eat well from His table while you discover your purpose. In the midst of the storms, you will find nourishment, strength, and peace because you are His, and He will never leave you nor forsake you.

God wants all of you, even that one thing you just can't seem to let go of. The part of you that feels too broken or insignificant to surrender. The thing you hold onto because you're afraid of what might happen if you let it go? God wants that, too. Every piece of your heart, every bit of your soul. When you surrender everything to Him— your past, your hurts, your fears, the storm, you unlock the freedom to walk fully in your calling, with Him ordering your steps through His Word daily.

Everything you've gone through, all the trials and challenges, has a purpose. There is purpose in your pain, purpose in your name, purpose in your birth, and purpose in your calling. As you begin to connect the dots, recognizing that each piece of your story has led you to this moment, you realize the confusion fades. There is no longer a conundrum. The puzzle is solved. No more mazes or dead ends, only a clear direction with your Father leading you to your true God-given purpose.

Finding your purpose starts with surrendering and seeking first the Kingdom of God to heal from whatever has broken you.

> Seek ye first the Kingdom of God and His righteousness and all of these things shall be added unto you.
>
> Matthew 6:33 (ESV)

That's everything you need to live out your purpose. If you are seeking God, you WILL find your purpose.

When I think about my Father God, who I get to call friend, the lover of my soul, my Redeemer, my Healer, my everything, my Savior, I get goosebumps. Yes, even in the dark storms of life, I think about Him because He is still good. Even in the storms. All the storms we have faced or will face in life are inevitable, but one thing is certain: we must prepare ourselves to stand firm and trust that God will get us through it. It is He who will give us the joy that we are looking for.

A Joy the World Can't Give

There's something so deeply satisfying about knowing you've touched someone's heart, helped them find their way, or lifted them when they were down. But what's even more incredible is the joy that fills your soul in the process—joy that isn't tied to circumstances or fleeting moments. It's a joy that the world didn't give, and trust me, the world can't take it away. It's a peace that surpasses all understanding, a quiet contentment that radiates from within, no matter what's happening around you. When you live with purpose and pour into the lives of others, you unlock a sense of fulfillment that no amount of wealth or recognition could ever replicate. It's the kind of joy that stays with you, growing stronger each time you give, each time you love, and each time you make a difference.

A Storm on Lakeshore Drive

Years ago, there was a violent and deadly winter storm on Lakeshore Drive in Chicago. The wind howled like a freight train and the snow fell in sheets, making it impossible to see.

As a woman in ministry, I poured myself into the work, serving, giving, preaching, teaching, writing and presenting Bible plays. That winter evening, I was fully immersed in doing His work, unaware of the happenings outside. And on that frigid night in Chicago, I found myself in a situation where all the knowledge and preparation in the world couldn't have helped me.

I became trapped in my car on Lakeshore Drive, caught in the middle of a brutal and relentless winter storm.

The storm came out of nowhere—a violent mix of hail, snow, and even lightning. I could hardly believe what was happening as the storm raged around me. Visibility was near zero, and my windshield wipers were useless against the thick sheet of ice that quickly covered my windows. My car crawled along, and I could see others around me struggling to move forward as well. Some cars were slipping, and others had slid completely off the road. I heard reports that people had drowned as the storm caused accidents and the lake surged onto the roadway.

But even in the midst of the chaos, I felt an overwhelming sense of peace. God's peace. It was as if God had been preparing me for this moment. I had a bag of groceries that my son left in the car from the night before by mistake, so that was my food. I had just filled up my gas tank. Not a coincidence. This was a God moment. Little did I know, those seemingly small actions were part of God's provision for me. The storm lasted hours, well into the night, and I couldn't see anything beyond the windshield. The weather was so severe that the ice on the road seemed impenetrable—and I was stuck, unable to move.

I called my family for comfort and to reassure them, though I had no idea just how grave the situation was. As I sat in the car, my stomach began to hurt, a sign I couldn't ignore. It wasn't until later that I learned the snow had accumulated around my car's exhaust pipe, and the carbon dioxide was slowly poisoning me. I was breathing it in, unaware of the danger.

I began to pray, asking God to help. Suddenly, I saw lights—the flashing beam of a fire truck's flashlight cutting through the storm. The firefighter was trying to make his way to us, but the snow was so deep on the roads that he couldn't get through. But that light was a beacon of hope, bringing with it a renewed sense of faith. I knew God was there. I was saved.

> "Through the fiercest storms of life, I was not alone. He had carried me once, and I knew He would carry me again."
>
> *crystal duncan-hogue*

When I finally made it home, my husband had prepared a hot bubble bath for me, a simple gesture of love and care. At that moment, it felt like a gift from heaven itself. I sank into that bath, feeling the warmth soak into my tired bones, my body and spirit recovering from the night's ordeal. I reflected on the storm and how God carried me through it. His grace, mercy and love had been my shield.

That night, I experienced God's protection and care in a way I'll never forget. And from that moment on, I knew, without a doubt, that no matter what storm came next— whether in ministry, in life, or in health—God would always be there to guide me through it. Through the fiercest storms of life, I was not alone. He had carried me once, and I knew He would carry me again.

My Health Attacked

As I reflect on my life, I see beauty and scars, the victories and the struggles. But I never imagined I'd have to endure the kind of physical suffering I've faced. So, I asked my Father, *Why? Why did You allow this suffering to happen to me? How can I fulfill the calling You placed on my life, to reach millions of people who need to know You, or better yet—how can I make a difference in my own community and across the globe if*

I am lying here in this hospital bed?

I remember this storm like it was yesterday. It was a life-threatening and sudden illness that required immediate medical attention. It was followed by treatments that stretched on for six months. The doctor looked at me and told me with a tone of finality, if I didn't get those treatments, there was a real possibility I could die from the severity of my illness.

Fear. It's what I felt when I heard those words. It shook me to my core. I thought, God, what's going on here? I've always been healthy. I've never had an illness like this before. In fact, this doesn't run in my family. I'm Your daughter—remember me? The one who uses all her gifts to serve and glorify you. The one You called into ministry to make a difference in communities. The one who edifies the body of Christ and builds up Your kingdom. The one who answered when You asked, "Who shall I send, and who will go for us?" I responded, "Lord, send me, I will go" (Isaiah 6:8, ESV).

And yet here I am, facing a storm I didn't expect.

As I wrestled with fear and confusion, I couldn't help but think of Jesus. Maybe He asked the same question: "Remember me, Lord? I'm Your Son, the one who came to save the world, yet I must suffer on this rugged cross while they mock Me and spit on Me." In that moment, Jesus heard them say, "If He is indeed the Christ, why not come down from the cross? Look! He saved others, but He can't even save Himself." There, He hung, naked, bloody, in excruciating pain. Yet even as He cried out to His Father, He knew it was all worth it in the end. He knew that He must die so we could live.

What an amazing love! To face the darkest of storms, knowing that the suffering would bring about a greater purpose. I thought, If Jesus could endure His storm for me, surely, I can endure mine for His glory. The storm may rage, the winds may howl, but through it all, His love remains. And that, my sisters, is a love that is worth everything. Yes, even the suffering.

The Suffering

I can still feel that needle sliding into my vein. I hated it. The discomfort, the cold rush of the medication, the feeling of helplessness. But I knew I had to get the treatments. I had to trust what the doctor said and trust God. The process was grueling, but it worked. Yet, as much as the medicine helped, I believe it was God doing the healing—His blood, His Word—that's what truly healed me. While I sat in that chair receiving treatment, I kept the Word of God close. The audio Bible played healing scriptures in my ear, verses about the healing blood of Jesus, and many other promises filled my mind. Listening to the scriptures took my focus off the discomfort and turned it toward the Healer. Jesus Christ. He healed me completely, and I believe He can heal you, too. Faith.

"If Jesus could endure His storm for me, surely, I can endure mine for His glory."

crystal duncan-hogue

> Many are the afflictions of the righteous, but the Lord delivers them from them all.
>
> Psalm 34:19 (ESV)

I held onto that promise, trusting that no matter what the affliction was, God would deliver me. And He did.

As long as we're in these earthly bodies, we are prone

to all kinds of illnesses, heartaches, and struggles. But I cling to hope and faith that one day, we will have new bodies in heaven—bodies free from pain, free from sickness, free from suffering. I have asked, "Lord, how can I go on? How can I fulfill the purpose You've called me to if my body doesn't work? I can't do the thing You created me to do. Before I was in my mother's womb, You formed me. So, what if my mind can't think, or my tongue can't speak, or my hands won't work, or my feet can't walk, or my lungs struggle to breathe? Father, I need You."

And every time I prayed, He came through for me. Through abuse, a bad diagnosis that caused fear, car accidents, loneliness, and longing—God has always been there. He never left me in the storm. He walked with me through every single trial, delivering me out of each, one by one.

Through all of my suffering, it made me think about Job. Job, a man who was righteous, one who feared God and shunned evil. He had everything—wealth, a family, and health. Yet, his life was shattered in an instant by a series of devastating storms. Job didn't just face loss—he lost his seven children in one day. His body was ravaged by painful sores, and he was left scraping his skin with broken pottery. On top of that, the woman by his side, his wife, told him to curse God and die as she watched him suffer.

And yet, Job, during unimaginable grief, falls down on his knees and worships God. In the face of tragedy, Job still recognized that the same God who gave him blessings also had the authority to allow suffering. Even though his body ached and his heart was broken, Job chose to worship the One who allowed the violent storm in his life.

This truth is both humbling and hard to grasp: God, in His sovereignty, holds all power. Even Satan, the enemy of our souls, must ask for permission before he can attack our lives. Whether it's our health, families, finances—or any area of our lives—God has the final say. Sometimes, like Job, God allows the storm. It's not because He doesn't love us, but because He knows there's purpose in the pain. He has a plan that we may not see at the moment. But it's there, and He is working behind the scenes.

Despite the storm that tore apart his world, Job fell down and worshiped God. He had his questions, just like we all do. I know I've asked my own. *Why God? Why now? When will the suffering end? Why is this storm so fierce? Why does it feel like it's never-ending?* Job had questions, too.

And maybe that's what we need to remember: it's okay to have questions, to wonder why the storms seem endless. I still have questions. Heck, I have more now than ever. But just like Job, I've learned that in the midst of the questions and pain, worship is still the answer. Job's worship didn't come from a place of understanding—it came from a place of trust. Trusting that God is still good, still in control, and still worthy of our praise—no matter how hard the storm.

In every moment of doubt, in every wave of fear, God has proven Himself faithful. And I know, as long as He is with me, I can keep moving forward, fulfilling the purpose He has for me. Even when the storms rage. He will deliver me, as He always has.

I've been through many more storms in my life—ones that left me broken, scarred, and questioning whether I could go on. There were times of physical abuse, when I was choked within an inch of my life, and Jesus stopped that man from taking my breath away. I think back to the car accidents, where it seemed as if my life was about to be snuffed out. But God halted the impact, sparing me. After surgery for a crushed knee, I came out singing, "I'm still holding on." And yes, He healed me. Completely.

When I look back at all the storms He brought me through, my heart swells with gratitude. I can't help but get up and dance, just like David did in 2 Samuel 6:15 (NLT). Because through it all, He's been my Savior, my Friend, my Protector, and my Healer.

And did I mention His name? Jesus Christ—the One who walks with me in the cool of the day (Genesis 3:8, KJV), just as He walked with Adam and Eve. The One who holds my hand, breathes life into me, and says, "Receive ye the Holy Spirit" (John 20:22, KJV). It's the Holy Spirit who comforts and empowers me for service.

Jesus, my Savior, walked on the water to meet me in the storm, but I had to get out the boat. He calls out to us, just as He called out to Peter on that stormy night, "Come to Me" (Matthew 14: 22-32, ESV). Imagine Peter, stepping out of that boat, walking toward the Savior, while the disciples—his friends—watched in disbelief, shouting, "Peter, what are you doing? Get back in the boat!" But Peter didn't listen to the doubters. He kept his eyes fixed on Jesus, and as long as he kept his focus on the One who walked on and created the water, he, too, could walk on water. As long as Jesus was with him.

But then the storm grew more intense. And as Peter's gaze wavered from Jesus to the storm, he began to sink. How many times have we done that—taken our eyes off Jesus and focused on the chaos around us? But even in our sinking, Jesus is still there. In fact, He reaches down, grabs hold of us, and says, "O you of little faith, why did you doubt?" (Matthew 14:31, ESV).

Would you be willing to step out of the boat into the storm if you knew Jesus was there waiting for you to come to Him? That's where we find our purpose. Stepping into the storm, trusting that God will equip us to do the work He has called us to.

My sister, there will be many storms in your life. As you search for your purpose, your calling, your destiny, know that God holds it all in His hands. He knows you; He hears your cry at night, and He cares deeply for you. He has called you by name.

Ephesians 2:10 (ESV) reminds us that we are God's handiwork, created in Christ Jesus to do good works, which He prepared in advance for us to do. All of us were created with a purpose—to do good works, to fulfill the calling God has on our lives. Yes, it gets hard sometimes, especially in the storms of life, but remember: God is with you. He sees you. He has created you for good work. And in those storms, you will find your God-given purpose.

I Found My Divine Purpose Through the Storms of Life

Along this journey called life, I found God. In my pain, rejection, health struggles, and in the many storms of life, God was always there. For didn't He say that He would never leave me nor forsake me? Oh yes, He did. I've heard His audible voice, seen a vision in the sky, felt His presence guiding me through every trial. And I saw His hand leading me, even when the path seemed unclear. It was in the midst of my deepest suffering that I discovered He was indeed with me.

I remember the moments when I could barely breathe through the storms. But even in those times, God would remind me of His promises. His Holy Spirit was always near, bringing the scriptures back to my remembrance, guiding my thoughts, and ordering my steps in His Word, day by day. As long as I stayed in His word, praying, praising Him and leaning on Him, I could find my way— no matter how dark the storm or how I felt emotionally. Even when I felt all alone, He was my constant companion, holding my hand and leading me toward the light.

Through His guidance, I've found peace. I've learned

to rest in His embrace, just like John did at the Last Supper, leaning on the Savior's chest and listening to His heartbeat. That's where I am now and it's clear, even though I still don't know or understand why certain storms came into my life. But each one has revealed more of God's plan for me.

The plan that God had for me has been far better than I could have ever imagined. I walked into a new chapter where my purpose wasn't defined by titles, my degrees, or accolades—but by the impact I could have on others. It became clear that true leadership wasn't about climbing higher, it was about serving others, inspiring them, and walking alongside them in faith.

When I finally surrendered everything I thought I was supposed to be to God, I discovered a passion and a fire that wouldn't go out. It just kept rising up within me. Even in the dark storms, I still had hope, faith, and trust that God would get me there with each step I took. I found the peace and joy I had been seeking for all those years.

So, I ask you, my friend, what is that thing that lights a fire in your soul? What is your passion? What would you do if money was no object and you could follow your heart wherever it led?

My sister in Christ, if God did it for me, He will do it for you, too. You may be in the middle of an unexpected storm right now, feeling lost, uncertain, or afraid. But I can promise you this: God will get you through it. You can discover your divine purpose in the storm. He will carry you through it, and you can walk with Him on the water, your eyes fixed on the One who created the storm, knowing He is guiding every step of your journey. Trust me, you are not alone. Jehovah Elohim, the God of the Universe, is leading you, just as He led me, toward your divine purpose through the storms.

Your purpose is not just a destination; it's a journey.

And even the storms have meaning. So, lean in. Let God lead. Watch as He transforms your life, one storm at a time. And if you don't know Jesus Christ, give your life to Him today. He is waiting for you with an outstretched arm (Deuteronomy 26:8, KJV).

Reflection

How did you respond during your storms of life? What actions did you take?

Are you seeking God through daily devotion, prayer, worship and scripture?

What are your next steps in discovering your God-given purpose?

_____

_____

_____

_____

_____

_____

_____

_____

_____

_____

_____

_____

_____

_____

_____

_____

_____

_____

Prayer to God

Heavenly Father, O Righteous Father, I come to You in the name of Jesus, giving You thanks for my sister who is reading this chapter. As she reflects upon the purpose You have for her life and every storm You have brought her through, may she recognize that You have been there all along. Yes, even through her pain, those dark and hurtful places, You were the light, guiding her footsteps towards You. Thanks for providing her with the strength she needs to get her through this storm. It's not an easy road, but as You got me through my storms, You can get her through hers. Lord, it's not a comfortable place for her, so please, give her the strength she needs at the very moment she feels she can't take it anymore. Let her lean on that strength to get her through. For when we are weak, yet we are strong in You.

Father, reveal to her Your divine purpose and plans for her life as she trusts You to get her through and walk by faith, clinging to Your love day by day. Order her steps through Your Word and guide her through Your Holy Spirit, bringing every scripture back to her remembrance.

Holy Spirit, comfort her and let her recognize Your presence and peace that surpasses all understanding during the storm. Father, You will get the glory out of her life through her testimony as she trusts in You, casting all her cares upon You, knowing that You care for her.

I ask these things in Jesus' name. Amen.

deepening your walk

Scripture Verse

"'For I know the plans that I have for you,' declares the Lord, 'plans for prosperity and not for disaster, to give you a future and a hope.'"

Jeremiah 29:11 (NASB)

Translations

Key Words

Context

Interpret

Application

crossroads in life

A Journey of Decisions, Challenges, and Faith

Francisca Etuokwu-Benyeogor

> If the axe is dull and he does not sharpen its edge, then he must exert more strength; but wisdom [to sharpen the axe] helps him succeed [with less effort].
>
> Ecclesiastes 10:10 (AMP)

Consider the word *crossroads*. What comes to mind? What signs do you see?

As I began to write this chapter, I pondered. And God reminded me of the "valley" experiences we all must face in life; those times when we face challenges, when things seem dark and the light is just out of reach.

Valley experiences will oftentimes take us to a crossroads where decisions must be made. Which path do you choose? And which direction will take you where God wants you to be?

Will you rise up and follow Him, trusting in faith? What choice will you make?

The Valley Experience

> Blessed is the man whose strength is in You, whose heart is set on pilgrimage. As they pass through the Valley of Baca, they make it a spring; the rain also covers it with pools. They go from strength to strength; each one appears before God in Zion.
>
> Psalm 84:5-7 (NIV)

In this scripture, the Psalmist acknowledges that even in valley experiences, our strength comes from God. The place of trusting Him in the most difficult seasons— especially with decisions, is crucial. We must trust His strength in unknown and uncertain places, and know He is with us and able to deliver us. Scripture shows God stepping into lowly places to promote, lead, heal, and build His people.

In the valley, we have moments where we desperately need direction, an answer, a word of encouragement. We send our petition to the Lord in prayer and meditation.

What might seem to be a delayed response from God can cause an overload of emotional, physical, and spiritual distress as we wait. The answer arrives late, and perhaps we ignore it. But God, who is ever-present in time of need, will show up with a solution that brings newness and a changed perspective of the situation.

His "lateness" does not mean it is over. It is all part of His plan (Jeremiah 29:11).

You must, with intention, see it through His lens to acknowledge His sovereignty in all his ways (Isaiah 43:19). He brings dead things to life and forgotten things into remembrance. Your case is not dead, but alive in Him who has power over death.

Our attitude in the waiting—our state of being—happy or sad, expectant or bitter—points to our heart posture and level of trust we have in the Father and His perfect timing and will for our lives.

To us, it may appear God is coming too late, as in the case of Martha and Mary. Martha said to Jesus, "If you were here, my brother would not have died." With love and compassion, Jesus told her Lazarus would live again. Martha had to see the One with resurrection power right in front of her in order to believe in her brother's complete healing (John 11:21).

We may be like Martha, feeling great disappointment and even pain in the waiting. Or we can choose to wait with our hands open, living in trust and obedience. Expectant hope.

As we journey in life, we come to pivotal moments— crossroads where decisions that will shape our future must be made. These moments, whether personal or spiritual, reflect times of trial, growth, and renewal. By exploring biblical figures like Naomi and Ruth, Esther, Deborah, and David, alongside modern women celebrities, we can find examples of navigating life's valley experiences and crossroads. And we learn and develop the capacity and understanding of the importance of faith, resilience, and purpose.

The Crossroads of Naomi and Ruth: A Journey of Redemption

Naomi's valley experience consisted of devastating losses—the death of her husband and sons. Naomi was left feeling bitter and questioning her purpose (Ruth 1:20-21, NIV). This was her crossroads, and she had to decide where to go. Naomi chose to return to Bethlehem, a decision that paved the way for redemption.

Naomi's daughter-in-law, Ruth, went through a valley experience alongside Naomi. And we see Ruth's crossroads decision very clearly in her famous biblical words, "Where you go, I will go; where you stay, I will stay" (Ruth 1:16, NIV), exemplify loyalty and courage. She left her homeland to follow Naomi, a journey into the unknown. That decision led Ruth and Naomi into God's divine plan. Ruth found favor, provision, and purpose in Boaz's field—ultimately becoming part of God's redemptive plan as an ancestor of Jesus.

In life, we come to a point where we must let go of our comfort zone to run the race of our God-given purpose.

Intersections and detours in life often require us to leave behind comfort for a greater purpose. Naomi and Ruth's story shows us we can trust God's providence, even in the valleys of life.

> "We learn to trust, knowing God has already gone ahead. Even in the unknown, God is preparing a new season."
>
> *francisca etuokwu-benyeogor*

We learn to acknowledge our losses—but not be defined by them. Naomi was heartbroken, but she moved forward. We must be open to new opportunities. Ruth never expected to find a new life, but she walked forward in faith.

We learn to trust, knowing God has already gone ahead. Even in the unknown, God is preparing a new season.

Esther's Crossroad: Choosing Courage Over Fear

Esther's journey included a valley of potential loss. She was a young Jewish woman who became queen in a foreign land. When her people faced extermination, she stood at a critical crossroads. Speaking to the king could cost her life, yet she knew silence would lead to her people's destruction (Esther 4:14, NIV).

Standing at the crossroads, Esther made a bold decision. With the guidance of her cousin, Mordecai, and faith in God, Esther declared, "If I perish, I perish" (Esther 4:16, NIV). Esther chose courage over fear. And her bravery led to the salvation of her people.

"At life's crossroads, courage rooted in faith can transform fear into victory."

francisca etuokwu benyeogor

At life's crossroads, courage rooted in faith can transform fear into victory. Esther's story reminds us that, sometimes, we are placed in situations "for such a time as this" (Esther 4:14, NIV).

Deborah: Leadership at the Crossroads

The story of Deborah took place in a valley of doubt.

As a judge and prophetess, Deborah stood at the crossroads of leadership during a time when women were rarely seen in positions of power. Faced with the oppression of her people, she rose as a leader who brought victory over their enemies (Judges 4:4-9, NIV).

Deborah empowered others; she partnered with Barak, encouraging him to lead Israel into battle. Her faith in God's plan emboldened Barak, proving that leadership at the crossroads often involves elevating others on our journey.

Through Deborah, we learn that leadership requires wisdom and faith, especially at critical crossroads. Her example shows us the importance of trusting God's guidance to inspire change, both in us and through us.

David: Crossroads and Restoration

David's life is an example of falling and rising again. David experienced betrayal, loss, and personal failure—yet, he always found his way back through his relationship with God.

One of the most defining moments in his life was at Ziklag (1 Samuel 30, NIV). After enemies raided his camp, burned everything, and took his family captive, David was distressed. And he had two choices—sink into despair or fight for restoration.

David chose to strengthen himself in the Lord. He pursued his enemies and recovered everything he lost.

WHAT CAN WE LEARN FROM DAVID?

We must encourage ourselves in the Lord (1 Samuel 30:6, NIV). We recall God's faithfulness. And we seek His divine direction.

We see David inquiring of the Lord before taking action. We pursue with faith. David didn't just pray; he took bold steps to restore and recover. And finally—trust that restoration is possible. What looks lost can be rebuilt in new ways through Him who makes all things possible.

Modern Crossroads: Women Celebrities

Oftentimes, we perceive celebrities' lives to be rosy, simply because they are celebrities. Yet they, just like us, go through times of struggles and challenges. Different moves and decisions may open new doors of opportunities—while also demanding their highest potential in learning and growing in their new spaces.

Whatever door is closed or opened places a demand to shift into new dimensions and levels of ability—and learning to thrive there.

Let's consider a few modern celebrities and their winding roads to impact, influence, and success.

OPRAH WINFREY

Oprah Winfrey faced significant obstacles growing up in poverty and surviving trauma. At the crossroads of her career, she chose authenticity and empathy, building a media empire while inspiring millions to embrace their journey. Coming from humble beginnings, Oprah overcame the odds and blazed a path for women in television, becoming an actress, producer, author, and extending her impact as an influential philanthropist.

SERENA WILLIAMS

Serena Williams is one of the greatest tennis players of all time, winning an amazing 23 Grand Slam singles titles, and revolutionizing women's tennis. Her crossroads involved balancing a demanding tennis career with motherhood, business aspirations, and philanthropic endeavors. Her story reflects resilience, perseverance, and the ability to redefine success in the role of a female athlete.

MAYA ANGELOU

Maya Angelou is much more than just an author. While she is known for her powerful autobiographical style of writing, she also made an unforgettable impact for Civil Rights and the resilience of black women. She turned pain into poetry and struggle into strength, inspiring many to rise above challenges with grace and courage. Her legacy reminds us that our voices matter, our stories have power, and "I am enough."

These modern women show us that valley experiences can be stepping stones to greatness when encountered with determination and vision. And crossroads can either be a place of confusion—or a springboard to success, influence, and impact.

COVID and Its Toll: Facing the Crossroads

The COVID-19 pandemic was more than a health crisis—it became a global valley experience, shaking economies, relationships, careers, and faith. Many people lost jobs, businesses collapsed, loved ones were lost, and life as we knew it was redefined.

The world itself was at a crossroads, and so were individuals.

For many, it became a season of deep self-reflection. Some were forced to start over, many struggled to find purpose, and others had to redefine success altogether.

When life's trajectory is interrupted, how do we rebuild? How do we regain our footing and move forward? The answers lie in faith, resilience, and the willingness to embrace change.

My Valley Experience and Crossroads

One of my valley experiences was a time of uncertainty. I felt stuck between where I was and where I wanted to be. My marital relationship was shaky. I was trying so hard to work on it. I had poured my heart into a path that seemed promising, but despite my efforts, progress felt slow and doors remained closed. Doubt began to creep in. I started seeing changes with my spouse; there were many arguments and changes in our relationship.

However, this challenging season gave birth to my first book, *The Waiting Game When God Stops the Clock.*

I began to question my purpose, wondering if I was on the right track. Had I missed my calling altogether?

I remember the fateful day that changed the trajectory of my life. I was crying, soaked in tears. And I heard the Lord say to me, "Arise and finish your book." I got up from the floor and began to write.

In the course of my writing, I had a peace that kept me focused. The Lord didn't stop in just telling to finish the book. He told me He would honor me in my writing. And yes, He certainly did. I won two awards for my book.

It was in that valley that I reached a crossroads decision—to either give up or press forward with faith. I chose to trust that delays were not denials, but divine preparation. Instead of dwelling on the obstacles, I began to see the lessons in the waiting. I refined my skills, deepened my faith, and surrendered my plans to God, knowing that His timing was perfect.

That decision changed everything. When the right door finally opened, I was stronger, wiser, and fully prepared to step into greater opportunities. The valley wasn't my setback—it was my training ground for my breakthrough.

Sometimes, the crossroads moments in life aren't about choosing the easiest path, but the ones that require faith, courage, and trust in God's plan.

> For I know the thought I have for you says the Lord a thought of peace and not of evil to bring you to an expected end.
>
> Jeremiah 29:11 (KJV)

And in the end, every valley leads to a mountaintop, establishing a walk with the Lord. The Lord is my El-Roi—the God who sees me.

1 Corinthians 2:9-10 (CSB) tells us, "But as it is written, What no eye has seen, no ear has heard, and no human heart has conceived—God has prepared these things for those who love him." I learned that no matter the adversities one is going through, there is always something better the Lord has in store for them.

Just trust Him!

"Sometimes, the crossroads moments in life aren't about choosing the easiest path, but the ones that require faith, courage, and trust in God's plan."

francisca etuokwu-benyeogor

Personal Valleys and Crossroads

Everyone faces valleys— loss, failure, or uncertainty. These moments often bring us to crossroads where faith and decisions intersect.

Reflecting on stories like Naomi and Ruth, Esther, Deborah, and David we see that the right path often involves faith—and trusting God even when the outcome is uncertain. It requires courage. Facing fears head-on with resilience. And it will often involve community and leaning on others for support and guidance.

The Biblical Promise at the Crossroad

God's Word offers comfort and assurance for us when we face life's crossroads:

> Trust in the Lord with all your heart and lean not on your own understanding; in all your ways submit to him, and he will make your paths straight.
>
> Proverbs 3:5-6 (NIV)

> Even though I walk through the darkest valley, I will fear no evil, for you are with me.
>
> Psalm 23:4 (NIV)

The crossroads in life are defining moments requiring faith, trust, wisdom, and courage. Whether through the valleys of Naomi, the boldness of Esther, the leadership of Deborah, the strength of David, or the resilience of modern women—we see that life's greatest victories often come from its greatest challenges.

By trusting God and embracing the unique or tailored lessons we learn from inspiring examples, we can navigate our own crossroads with confidence, love, discipline and purpose.

What do you see when you are on a crossroad?

I see 1 Peter 2:9 (CSB), which says:

> But you are a chosen race, a royal priesthood, a holy nation, a people for his possession, so that you may proclaim the praises of the one who called you out of darkness into his marvelous light.

I see the picture of God's greatness poured into us for our journeys in this life. We are wonderfully and fearfully made to showcase forth His glory.

We are called to press forth, breaking the ceiling and taking our rightful position.

Conclusion

A word of encouragement for you.

Your valley experience is not your final destination. Always remember God is with you and He is strengthening you for the journey ahead. Build your trust in Him, continually lean into His wisdom, and allow Him to turn your valley into a place of growth, renewal, and transformation. You are moving from strength to strength, and very soon, you will step into your place of divine fulfillment.

Moving Forward with Trust and Courage

There is a saying that we are creatures of habit—constantly moving, seeking comfort, and avoiding difficulty.

However, valley experiences teach us that growth happens outside our comfort zones.

- What if your valley experience is not a setback, but

rather a setup for something greater?

- What if the hardship you are facing is the foundation for your breakthrough?
- What if, instead of running from the valley, you embraced it as a place of divine transformation?

Decree

I rise from every shackle and limitation that has held me down in Jesus name. I take judicial authority, rendering the plans of the enemy useless. I stand on God's great promises.

I may stand at the crossroads, but I am not lost. I decree that divine wisdom and clarity guide my steps. The path before me is illuminated with God's truth, and I will not be led by fear or confusion. Every decision I make aligns with God's perfect will, and no weapon formed against my destiny shall prosper.

Declaration

I declare that I am stepping forward with boldness and confidence! I am equipped, empowered, and strengthened for the road ahead. The Lord is my shepherd, and He leads me in the way I should go. I declare that confusion has no power over me. My mind is clear, my spirit is steadfast, and my heart is anchored in faith. The Lord has not given me a spirit of fear but of love and sound mind! I trust that every choice I make is divinely ordered, and I will not be shaken. God walks with me, His voice directs me, and His presence surrounds me. My future is secure, my purpose is unfolding, and my breakthrough is near!

Reflection

Prayer to God

I pray you embrace faith, courage, and discernment as doors of opportunity open before you, and distractions are removed from your path. May you walk in God's timing, favor, and purpose, and live in His best season for your life. May you reject every spirit of fear, doubt, and delay that seeks to paralyze your movement. I pray you break free from indecision, stagnation, and the weight of your past. No longer will you look backward in regret, nor will you remain stuck in uncertainty. Instead, may you embrace God's direction, supernatural wisdom, and undeniable favor.

In Jesus' name, Amen.

deepening your walk

Scripture Verse

"Blessed is the man whose strength is in You, whose heart is set on pilgrimage. As they pass through the Valley of Baca, they make it a spring; the rain also covers it with pools. They go from strength to strength; each one appears before God in Zion."

Psalm 84:5-7 (NIV)

Translations

Key Words

Context

Interpret

Application

your call

Lori L. Dixon, Ed.S.

Dear *Elevating Wisdom on the Walk* Reader,

In these days we are living, you have witnessed greater revival than in past days. As you know, we are having powerful challenges and traumas, but we have a God who loves us through it all and in each step we take. Thank you for choosing to read this book and hear the stories of six women who believed and answered the Lord's calling to write for YOU.

You have read the deep stories of faith, loss, joy, healing, surrender, and transformation in the pages of this book. Many of the stories you have read from our women include their testimony of faith, too.

Which ones have touched your heart? Which one

caused you to hear the Holy Spirit speaking to you? Which one aligned with your life circumstance now or even before?

You may be asking, "How do I give my life to Christ and what does that mean?" Are you feeling the nudging of the Holy Spirit to accept Christ into your life and into your heart? There is no age, time, place or certain words to say in this interaction with the Lord. It all begins with a simple understanding and a prayer of acceptance and surrendering of your life to Him. You receive the ability to see clearer the wisdom God gave you back in the Garden of Eden and to begin communing with Him again. You also open the door to letting Christ into your heart where He will never leave. He lives inside of us and walks with us every day.

Declaration

Begin by saying something like, "I believe in God the Father and in Jesus Christ, His Son. I am ready to begin a walk of faith today. I am inviting Christ into my heart."

> For everyone who calls on the name of the Lord will be saved.
>
> Romans 10:13 (TPT)

Prayer of Surrender

Using this as a guide, pray with a sincere heart:

Dear Father God, I come before You today with a heart filled with faith and love. I surrender my life—all of it, to You. I believe Jesus Christ was born free of sin, died on the cross for me and my sins, and rose from the grave three days later, I believe in Your beautiful gift of salvation, grace, and eternal life because of the sacrifice of Jesus Christ.

Lord, today I repent and turn from my old life. Your grace and mercy bring me to begin walking with a childlike faith. Today, in this moment, I ask you for a new life in which Jesus Christ and the Holy Spirit are within me. Thank you, God, for forgiving me and wiping away my sin away to become brand new in You.

In Jesus' Holy and precious name, Amen.

There is so much I want to share with you about this new walk of faith and how YOU become a sister or brother in the family of God. We are His children.

Will you choose to be a part of the family? We can't wait to greet you and walk with you. You may choose to reach out to one of the authors or to one of us in the WoW Team. We would also love for you to join our Facebook community called, "Wisdom on the Walk Author community" and share your testimony with us. We also have events and prayer team zoom calls together as a community of Christian women. Being with others on this journey is important.

I suggest a few that I love below. Then, begin reading the scriptures shared with you in each of the chapters. Open your heart and let God speak truth into your life... today.

You may want to reach out and obtain the new "Deepening the Walk" journal and scripture mapping complimentary PDF. It is also available for a print copy on Amazon.

- **King James Version (KJV):** Great for memorizing verses

- **New International Version (NIV):** Easier to read in everyday language

- **The Passion Translation (TPT):** My favorite for connection to your life and sharing with others; only in New Testament, Proverbs, and Psalms at this time, with smaller books just for the Old Testament

If you prayed this prayer and asked Christ into your heart, please reach out to us. We want to pray for you and invite you to join us in our retreats, prayer team, bible studies, and more.

meet the authors

Have you read their stories yet? Maybe you turned to the back pages to find out more about these authors. It doesn't matter how you ended up on this part of the book, but it is essential that you did. If I could create an invitation for you to converse with each author in this new book of the series, I would. Faith-filled, Christ-centered, Spirit-led, God-directed, and Purpose-driven women authors who are dedicated to sharing their stories with you.

Why? They want to influence your walk with God and strengthen how a personal relationship with Him can be a pivotal moment in your life. They write for you and with you as a "real" person, having moments that matter. Each woman prayed and asked God which story from their life and learning path would create the most profound influence in the world for God's Kingdom to take root and grow. I can't wait for you to meet them.

"Meet the Authors" sounds so stuffy. If you haven't felt the connection between these women, you will. They are my "sisters" in faith… in Christ… in outreach, and many other unique situations and circumstances. They are co-authors in this book, yet that feels sterile and labeled again. As I said, they are my "sisters" in writing, support, and connection.

In 2023, God asked me to write another book, and you may already know how he called twelve women. We created an academy, community, and retreat to assist them in transformational writing, editing, social media, business outreach, and growth, which became the second book in our series, *Embracing Wisdom on the Walk*. For me and many of those women, it was a journey together of faith and much more. God asked me to continue publishing and writing for these women and many others. He placed a continued "calling" on my life to build more for Him and His Kingdom. There are days I feel like Noah, with no idea of what I am creating, what it will look like, how it will impact and influence our world, and who will enter this ark for the adventure He destined for each of us individually and collectively.

Our newest book in the series, *Elevating the Wisdom on the Walk*, brings a new group of authors, which includes two returning authors from the second WoW book.

These beautiful women have grown together, learned, written, shared, connected, supported, and focused on their lives, work, families, and walked with wisdom through the journey together. They conquered fears, broke free of shackles, laughed at their "old" selves, and praised the Lord through it all.

On the next series of pages, you will find the biographies of these powerful women. I challenge you to: meet them, celebrate them, listen to them, and connect with them. You will be glad you did; I know I AM!

If you are interested in books, information on authoring with us, or events:

- Reach out to **lori@walkwithlori.com**
- Go to our website at **www.walkwithlori.com**

Be Blessed, Be Bold, Be YOU!

Lori

niki banning

NIKI BANNING is a Jesus-loving wife, mom, and Yaya.

She is a certified CORE Coach, and has been blessed to see her business, *NikiB Virtual Services*, blossom since starting in 2020. She has found a reignited passion for writing and editing, which led to Niki becoming a published author and launching *Story Guardian Editing Services*.

Through involvement first as a Caregiver and then as a leader for Stephen Ministry, Niki found her passion and calling: to come alongside others in support, and uplift them in business and life. But more importantly, she loves to encourage others in their personal relationship with God.

Niki is a relationship-builder, advocate, and ally. She has the ability to help others calm the chaos of their business and be a trusted partner and right hand. You can find Niki in her office, usually wearing fuzzy socks and accompanied by her also fuzzy office dog, Ruby.

nikibvirtualservices.com

Facebook: @nikibanning and @nikibvirtualservices

Instagram: @nikibanning

natalie merrill

NATALIE MERRILL is an author with a tender heart for prodigals. She is blessed to be the Director of Small Groups for *Alive at Last*, a non-profit organization working with traumatized, trafficked, and domestically abused women.

Natalie's most cherished title and job description is that of Mommy. Natalie's husband loves to describe her as sincere, fiercely loyal, caring, and compassionate.

Natalie enjoys social dancing and keeping fit. She has an associate degree in marketing, and enjoys being able to use her God-given creativity when she can.

Most of all, Natalie loves fellowship with brothers and sisters in Christ through Bible studies and everyday encounters. One of her favorite sayings is, "I love it when we all shine together!"

Join Natalie and learn how she found the depth of Jesus' compassionate grace through her own prodigal journey. You can connect with Natalie at authornataliemerrill@gmail.com.

tina jacobson

TINA JACOBSON is an author, speaker, and the visionary founder of Version of You by Tina. As a business and personal growth coach, she helps business owners and management teams unleash their full potential to become impactful leaders and mentors.

With extensive experience in Human Resources, business development, and management, Tina brings over 25 years of experience to support individuals and teams in achieving success.

In addition to coaching, Tina is proud to be a mom of one and Nonna to two beautiful grandchildren. As a health and personal growth mentor, Tina is dedicated to helping people live and lead with purpose, and find the very best version of themselves.

You can connect with Tina at *versionofyoubytina.com.*

mantequilla green

MANTEQUILLA GREEN is a best-selling author. She was featured in *Embracing Wisdom on the Walk*, which was released in April 2024.

As an educator of 25 years, Mantequilla has served in a myriad of roles, including teaching, mentoring, and leadership within the public school system. Presently, she serves as an administrator at a middle school in Austin, Texas. Mantequilla is an inspiration to her students and peers, and is a past recipient of the highly respected Teacher of the Year award.

Along with being a doctoral candidate, she also holds a Master's in Education and two Bachelor's degrees in Psychology and Communications (Journalism).

In her spare time, Mantequilla enjoys cooking, traveling, reading, and attending her local church. She can be reached at mshaleighgreen@hotmail.com.

crystal duncan-hogue

CRYSTAL DUNCAN-HOGUE is the Founder and CEO of CHM Bible Theatre, a nonprofit organization that fosters faith-based arts, theater, and leadership programs. Her mission is to orchestrate innovative and inspirational Bible stage plays for communities, enriched by culturally sensitive educational youth programming.

Crystal is a speaker, author, and an executive coach for Crystal Clear Coaching, helping other leaders of nonprofits. She is a playwright, artistic director, singer, songwriter, and wears many hats as a leader, wife, and mother. Crystal has cultivated meaningful connections across diverse spheres of the community, receiving several awards for community impact.

Crystal holds a bachelor's degree in theology and a master's degree in business administration. She also holds teaching and ministerial licenses. Driven by unwavering commitment, Crystal directs her multifaceted talents towards positively impacting society and encourages others to do the same.

She is happily married to Charles, a school principal. Together, they have raised three adult children. Her passion for life, the Bible, and serving others drives her leadership. Crystal aims to inspire unity, hope, and faith while fostering healing in communities.

You can find Crystal at:

www.chmbibletheatre.org

www.crystalclearcoach.org

Connect with Crystal at chmbtceo@gmail.com.

francisca etuokwu-benyeogor

FRANCISCA ETUOKWU-BENYEOGOR is is a Dallas resident, entrepreneur, Apostle, and founder of Armor of God Healing Ministries with the mission and vision to help, heal, and restore hope. Her Kingdom mandate is to impact lives globally with the transforming Word of God.

Francisca is author of an award-winning book, *The Waiting Game: When God Stops the Clock*. She is a transformational mental health coach and producer of Just One Word Show, which helps others experience God's glory and figure out "One Word" that will help shape their lives. Francisca has been featured in productions such as *The Voyage Dallas* and *The Whole Woman* magazines. As a servant leader, Francisca is a woman of grace, impact, and purpose, transforming lives globally with *Just One Word* through multiple platforms and speaking engagements.

Francisca's love for the Lord is contagious. Her hobbies include art, writing, fashion, music, and love for people. However, her greatest desire is to fulfill her God-given purpose.

Learn more about Dr. Francisca and her ministries at www.aoghm.org and email her at authorfrancisca32@gmail.com.

Wisdom on the Walk (WoW) book series, academy, and community!

Spirit-filled, Christ-centered, God-directed Life Stories

Has God specifically chosen YOU to be part of a new project to bring forth God's purpose in our lives? YOU are invited to join us in the next book in the WoW book series, as we share stories in this meaningful way. It is more than a book; it is an interactive journey of reflection, creativity, learning, connecting, and embracing God's work to influence and impact others. Your story will be intertwined with the writing of best-selling Lori L. Dixon, designs to engage you in furthering your purpose, and areas to reflect on His word in your own life.

I love how God has designed the expansion with further books, an academy of learning and writing, and an online community for sisterhood. What a beautiful and meaningful way to further HIS Kingdom by creating circles of disciples for unique and powerful purposes. As you will experience, we have workshops, prayer team circles, retreats, partners in writing, and engage in time together, sharing information, stories, insights, support, faith, and growth moments.

Welcome to the Wisdom on the Walk Author Journey!

Here are some quick items to know about the experience:

- We meet monthly for 9-12 months.
- Each session includes mentoring, learning, connection, interaction with other authors, bible study, and prayer. You will also have a 1:1 coaching session each month for guidance and direction in your writing, faith walk, social media presence, marketing, media, and more!
- Upcoming retreats in Dallas and beyond are planned for 2024 already.
- Further opportunities for sponsoring, speaking, and writing your own book are available.

Meet our LLD Legacy Publishing and Media Team:

Lori Dixon
owner, author, and your visionary leader in the process

Niki Banning
best-selling author, assistant, and leading editor

Callie Revell
publishing assistant, graphic design, and support

Do you hear that? A call to action. Are you feeling God is calling YOU? Have you ever thought He wants you to share your life story, healing, transformation, and insights with other women and glorify His work in YOU?

Your Story **is waiting to be told.**

Contact us for more information about the WoW Journey or to publish your book with us!

meet Lori L. Dixon

@walkwithlori
@lorilanedixon

Lori L. Dixon, Ed.S. is a Visionary and Epiphany Expert with her business ventures, LLD Legacy Publishing, LLC, and Walk with Lori. Lori brings more than 4 decades of wisdom and experience working in education, therapies, business, and nonprofits. She is a best-selling author and publisher, thera-coach, speaker, and a multiple international award-winning host and producer on TV. With her dynamic television appearances on Bravo's Real Housewives of Dallas, Lori understands the 'reality' of how the next chapter of life may be rewritten at any time. She may now be watched internationally on TV as a co-host on Lite It Up TV and Sawubona...I SEE You on ZondraTV Network on ROKU, AmazonFire, Chromecast, and iTunes.

Lori believes in finding the "heartstrings" in life, releasing the strongholds of fear, and living the life God has designed for you. As a writer for many years and a published author, editor, and frequent media influencer for others, Lori knew her passion would always be in the "stories" of our lives. She expanded her mission for writing and publishing with her own Christ-centered, faith-filled books, numerous compilations, and children's books. Lori believes we are all SEEN in our own God-given divine design and that we have a mission to share it right now within the world.

Through LLD Legacy Publishing, LLC, which is a full-service publishing company with editing, writing, illustrating, design, media, and marketing, she brings her passions together for each author. Her newest program, Wisdom on the Walk (WoW) is a unique experiential journey for women to become authors and further their own stories and missions for others.

Walk with Lori

VISIONARY LEADER

LORI L. DIXON, Ed.S.

Founder and Owner, LLD Legacy and Walk with Lori

TheraCoach, Publisher
International Multiple Award-Winning Host and Producer

469-855-0287
www.walkwithlori.com
lori@walkwithlori.com

Did you gain wisdom on your walk?
Order more copies to pour into others!

www.walkwithlori.com/wisdomonwalk

or scan this code with your phone: